SNIPER POCKET BOOK

written & illustrated by
Frank Fletcher, Rupert Godesen

production and published by
Military Pocket Book Ltd.

Military Pocket Books Ltd
PO Box 28, Leven Beverley
East Yorkshire
HU17 5LA
UK
www.milpkbk.co.uk

INTRODUCTION

The aim of this book is to give the reader an insight into the world of the Military Sniper and as to provide a reference guide to both Snipers and Sharpshooters themselves.

At times I have elaborated and tried to make clear some of the lesser understood points and to separate fact from fiction.

I must also point out that although useful this book is only a guide and skill in these subjects must be learnt from practice and actual time spent shooting.

What is not mentioned is anything deemed sensitive and operational directed. For this the sniper must refer to his own unit SOPs and advice from his unit Master Sniper/Sniper Instructor.

To this end some of the meat is purposely missing, but hopefully this book will provide the template for learning and the platform to build upon.

To those non-snipers out there, I hope that you find this book both interesting and enlightening. On today's battlefields the snipers are truly a breed apart. Not only shaping the battlefield and destroying the enemies command and control ability but by keeping his comrades alive by providing the "Sniper Umbrella" thus neutralizing enemy snipers and threats at long range. It is a fact that the snipers enjoy the rewards of their prowess and all are dedicated professionals taking great satisfaction in a job well done.

It is true of the old adage to their enemy of today,

"Don't run you will only die tired!"

CONTENTS

History of the British Sniper
The Origins of the Sniper, Early Days, The Napoleonic War, Advances in Bullet Design, The 20th Century, The First World War, World War Two, Post World War Two, Birth of the L96, Future Weapons - Today.

Command, Organisation Tasks and Role
Background, Role and Task, Platoon Commander, Platoon 2ic, Section Commander, Sniper (No1), Sniper (No2), Task, Principles of Employment, Uses in Phases of War.

Sniper Marksmanship
The Bullet, The Case, The Primer, The Barrel, Rifle Barrel - Named Parts, Firing Action, Harmonics, Jump Angle, The 'Cold Bore' Shot, Arc of Bullet Trajectory, External Ballistics, Culmination Point, Principles of Good Shooting, Positional Testing and Adjusting, Types of Trigger Control, Factors that Determine Good Trigger Control, Schmidt & Bender 5-25 x 56 PMII, Schmidt & Bender 3-12 x 50 PMII, Correct Sight Alignment Angular Shift Error, Other Conditions that could affect The Shot, Poor Shooting, Miss Drill, Alternative Shooting Positions, Sling Supported, Definition of a Group, Range to Target, The Cosine Method Formula, Rifle Cleaning.

Sniper Fieldcraft
Introduction, The Aim of Camouflage, Why things are Seen, The Ghillie Jacket, The Ghillie Shroud, Making up the Ghillie Suit, Stalking, The Drag Bag, Planning, Action on The Stalk, Types of Cover En Route to your FFP, Route Selection, Principles Effecting Movement, Withdrawal/Extraction, Sub-Surface Hide, Sniper Sub-Surface Hides, Enlarged Fire Trench, Semi-Permanent Hide,

Observation Post, Disadvantages, Viewing & Firing Apertures, The OP Log, Area Search, Orders and Rehearsals.

Judging Distance
Target Detection, Training the Eye, Light, Observation Procedures, Maintaining Observation, Scanning and Searching, Night Adaptation, The Crack & Thump Method, Shot Analysis, Sniper Thermal Image Capability, Method of Indication of Targets, After Action, Reason for Indexing, Sniper Priority Target List, The Unit of Measure, Other Devices.

Panoramic Sketching
What is a Panoramic Sketch? Uses of The Sketch, Principles, Building the Panoramic Sketch, Adding Detail and Shading, Summary.

Air Photography
Introduction, Use of Air Photography, Tactical use of Air Photography on Operations, Scaling Air Photography, Photo/Map Comparison, Stereoscopy.

8 Longest Sniper Shots in History
Introduction, No. 8: Staff Sergeant Jim Gilliland's, No. 7: Unknown Norwegian Sniper, No. 6 Corporal Christopher Reynolds, No. 5 Gunnery Sergeant Carlos Hatchcock, No. 4 Sergeant Brian Kremer, No. 3 Master Corporal Arron Perry, No. 2 Corporal Rob Furlong, No.1 Corporal of Horse Craig Harrison.

Summary - Question & Answer Session with the Author

HISTORY OF THE BRITISH ARMY SNIPER

THE ORIGINS OF THE SNIPER

In India during the late 18th century British Army Officers stationed there used to wile away their leisure time hunting a game bird that was both small and nimble, their quarry was called the **"Snipe."** Due to its small size and agility it was a very difficult target to engage and shoot.

Before long, the term **"Sniper"** was used to describe a skilful hunter well versed in the art of both shooting and stalking. The earliest recorded instance of the word "Sniping" was found in a letter sent home from India in 1770, it read "the soldiers put their hats on the parapet for the enemy to shoot at and humorously called it sniping."

Although the word sniper and sniping was at that time generally confined to the British Army and the English-speaking world, accurate rifle fire at selected individuals was initially called "Sharpshooting". It wasn't really until the 20th century that Sniping came to describe a specific military activity.

History of the British Sniper

The British Army's Sharpshooter Rifle, a UOR during the recent Afghan campaign.

The sniper is not just a sharpshooter (an accurate shot) he is in fact a highly trained specialist trained in a wide variety of fighting disciplines, that will help him achieve his commanders mission as well as keeping him alive when he's hard pressed.

His primary function is to get himself in to a position in order to kill selected high-value targets (HVT) at long ranges in all weathers and during all phases of war.

The sharpshooter however is no more than a trained Rifleman who is an opportunist and takes careful shots at the enemy when the chance arises. Nowadays this soldier is called the "Dedicated Marksman" and he is trained and equipped accordingly.

EARLY DAYS

The origins of sniping date back to the 18th Century when rifles were first used in the precision attack role. It must be mentioned that the concept of rifling, which is the cutting of spiral grooves in the bore of a rifle therefore spinning the projectile, was nothing new.

Gunsmiths had been aware of this technique from as early as the 16th Century. The problem lay in the design of the projectile and traditionally this in turn had to be rammed into the bore to enable the rifling to work. It was a time consuming affair and unpopular.

Later the introduction of a greased patch wrapped around the ball projectile would make the process faster but a true sharpshooting rifle was still a long a way off.

Although individual sharpshooting rifles had been used in the earlier wars between the British and the French, the potential of sharpshooters was never fully understood until the American Revolutionary War (1775 -1783).

The British Army learned the hard way and after being outshot by American civilians they set about employing their own sharpshooters. By the end of the War they had a purpose built rifle and skirmishers of their own.

THE NAPOLEONIC WAR

As the result of experiences gained in North Africa, the British Army took up the rifle again during the Napoleonic Wars (1792 to 1850). The 95th Rifles, who had distinguished themselves fighting the French in Spain, later made famous on TV as "Sharpes Rifles" were given the Baker Rifle.

This was the rifle supplied by the English gunsmith, Ezekiel Baker. The Baker rifle had indeed won the National Trial held at Woolwich in 1800, outperforming rifles from both America and Europe and consequently was found to be the most suitable for military use. It was well made, durable and could fire two sizes of ball, the larger for conventional rifle shooting, the smaller operating as a smooth bore for rapid fire at close ranges.

When firing the larger conventional ball the user could engage targets with precision at 200 yards. With skill and favourable conditions targets could be engaged at ranges out to 500 yards

although in practice this normally averaged 300 yards.

In 1808 Tom Plunkett, a Rifleman in the 95th Rifles shot and killed General Colbert of the French Army with a single shot. Plunkett had identified and singled out the General as a high-value target and took him down accordingly.

Throughout the campaign the 95th Rifles earned a reputation for themselves as an elite unit in the British Army. Unlike the rest of the Army they were kitted out in green and black and fought out in front as skirmishers, using both cover and superior single shot firepower to great effect.

It was later recorded that at the Siege of Badajos a battery of French Artillery was silenced by such action.

ADVANCES IN BULLET DESIGN

Alexander Forsyth led the way with his invention of the percussion cap. The great advantage of the percussion-lock system was that it was fully enclosed and resistant to the effects of the weather.

The British Army was keen to test its potential and as a result during

> Historians claim that, when Oliver Cromwell's troops were about to cross a river to attack the enemy, he addressed them with a rousing speech concluding *'put your trust in God; but mind to **keep your powder dry'**.* In these modern times with our hi-tech weapons systems we have little appreciation of just how hard this must have been to accomplish.

trials held in 1834, it became the standard system amongst the leading military nations of the day. Subsequently it was adopted and became the priming element of the modern rifle cartridge.

This meant that although the percussion cap gave improved reliability, the question of speeding up the rifles reloading process remained unanswered. The answer came in the form of a new bullet designed by a Frenchman, Captain Claude Minié.

The Minié bullet was cylindroconical in shape, with a hollowed out base. It was smaller than the bore of the rifle and easily chambered, but when the charge was fired the force of the expanding gases entered the hollowed out base, expanding the bullet so that it locked into the grooves of the rifling and it was driven forward with increased accuracy.

It was so successful that it was used by both the British and French in the Crimean War and later by both sides in the American Civil War. Improvements in gunpowder composition allowed both greater consistency and power needed for longer range shooting.

Now with the right tool in the hands of a skilled firer, targets could be engaged and killed at ranges in excess of half a mile. Leaps in technology meant that the day of the sniper was almost at hand.

THE 20TH CENTURY

Learning the hard way from being outshot and out skirmished by the African Kommando units during the Boer War, the British Army had some catching up to do. Out went the Red Coats' famous Crimson Tunics and in came the Khaki Drab Battledress that would remain for much of the 20th Century.

At home establishments such as The National Shooting Centre at Bisley, Surrey were created to provide a centre of excellence for individual marksmanship and at last the Army was on the right path.

THE FIRST WORLD WAR

Sniping as we know it was born in the stagnant hell of WWI trench warfare.

The Germans began the war with around 20,000 scoped rifles and by skilful deployment of their snipers and sharpshooters they created fear and panic in the British lines. At their peak they were killing 60 British Soldiers a day.

To counter this menace Britain needed its own snipers, yet at the start of the war they only had an odd assortment of around 850 scoped and suitable rifles. Something had to be done.

In 1916 Major Hesketh-Pritchard formed the first Sniping, Observation and Scouting School (SOS). He was convinced that through patient study of the German Sniper and his tactics a counter could be achieved.

To help achieve this the **Lovat Scouts** were seconded to him to assist in the training. They brought with them the observational skills learnt as Ghillies, stalking deer in the Highlands of Scotland and were experts in this field.

They introduced the **"Ghillie Suit"** which was based upon the drab clothes they wore when stalking, coupled with the excellent Scout Regiment Telescope this gave the concealed observers the edge over their German counterparts.

German snipers would normally operate individually and it was quickly realised that to defeat them would take both time and patience. To achieve this two men were needed, one man acting as the observer and the other the shooter. The latter would be armed with a decent scoped rifle and some advanced marksmanship training. The **"Sniper Pair"** was thus born.

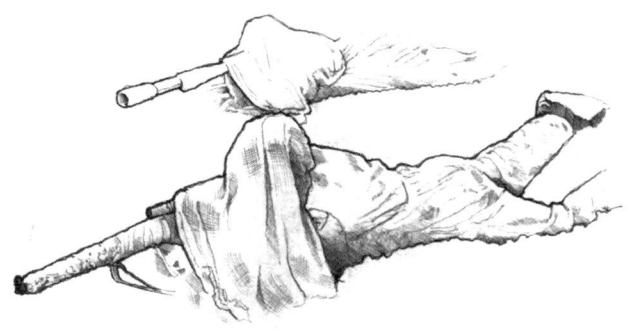

When the sniper pairs went into the line against the Germans in mid 1916 the inevitable "cat and mouse game" began. A German tactic would be to use snipers to keep their enemies heads down in the trenches when they conducted attacks.

The Germans also used their infantry squads to protect the sniper positions when the snipers were in more open terrain. The British Army had by contrast put a greater emphasis on field craft and camouflage in their sniper training and this started to pay off.

As German snipers became more prone to attack by British snipers, the Germans started using steel plates to protect themselves from counter sniper fire. The Germans would either use steel plates as body armour or place a steel plate with a loophole in front of the sniper position to observe and fire from.

Since the Germans were using armour plating to protect themselves, newer bullet technology was needed to defeat them. The British Army snipers then started using longer range heavier projectiles to defeat the armour, such as the .450 calibre used by hunters to bring down elephants. And later this was replaced by the Armour Piercing bullet.

Snipers and infantry units working in the trenches also started using more deception to lure out enemy snipers and so fix their locations. The use of fake positions and mannequins of all sorts were used.

The "cat and mouse" sniper duels went on for over a year along the western front, tactics drove improvements in technology and vice versa. In fact although never totally defeated, by the middle of 1917 the role had been reversed and the German Sniper menace was subdued.

It is a fact that many of the techniques and training of snipers that we use today were developed from World War One and still have relevance. In fact six of the seven sniper skills taught and required today were taken direct from the 1916 Sniper Training Manual. The British Sniper Pair as we know him today was born.

WORLD WAR TWO

During the Second World War despite the passing of just 21 years, it looked as though the hard learned lessons from the trenches had almost been forgotten. As before skills had to be re-learned and Sniping Schools established yet again. The Lee Enfield No4 Mk1 was chosen as the tool and this variant included a 3.5 power scope, the No 32.

The combination was called the No4 (T). The Airborne Camouflaged Denison Smock was made available to the snipers and most were suitably equipped. Not all sniping groups used the "Sniper Pair" and as before those who employed the duo were often more effective.

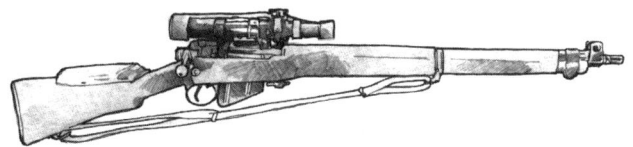

Even the Germans had failed to readdress their failing in the First World War, often using solitary snipers. It was during this time that some famous snipers entered the history books.

The likes of Finnish sniper **Simo Häyhä** nicknamed *"The White Death"* notching up 505 kills against the invading Russian forces and later the Russian sniper Sergeant Major Vassili Zaitsev, in Stalingrad. Made famous by the film "Enemy at the gates".

The famous duel between him and a Top German Sniper Officer was much documented although historically never confirmed by the Germans. Upon the conclusion of the War in 1945 the sniper had not really advanced much more than in WW1.

POST WORLD WAR TWO
Snipers were used again in Korea and on every subsequent Operational Deployment that the British Military took part in.

The Royal Marines set up a full time training establishment for their own snipers and in the Army snipers would be trained at unit level by Sniper Instructors who had attended the Infantry Sniper Commanders Course.

Snipers were also employed within the Royal Air Force forming part of the fighting capability of the RAF Regiment. The establishment of snipers would often depend on the requirements of the unit and for most snipers it was an uphill struggle for resources to train and maintain their skills between operations.

This was very much the case during the Falkland War in 1982. Argentinian snipers were armed with far superior weapons and US made night vision devices, the British snipers fell back on their excellent training and skills to defeat them.

The L42A1 that the British snipers were using was well past its sell by date. It was still a throwback to the last of the Lee Enfield Rifles and was still fitted with the same No 32 scope, the only change being that it was recalibrated in metres and not yards.

BIRTH OF THE L96

Returning from the Falklands War, the British Army, although triumphant, had a lot of equipment deficiencies and failings to address. For the snipers this meant a new sniper rifle. It was at this time that a unique partnership was taking place in the world of UK

The picture shows the L96A1 circa 1999 after the "Mid Life Upgrade" fitment of the Schmidt and Bender 3-12x50 Rifle Scope. This scope replaced the original 6x fixed power scope

Rifle Shooting. Being a left hander Dave Walls, built himself a target rifle using all the features he thought were the best available in the mid 1970's. Along with his shooting companion and fellow engineer Dave Caig, they set up a part time business making shooting accessories for Target Shooting rifles being used at both County and National Level. This was based upon the fact that they were both tired of using weapons that were not robust enough, even just for target shooting. During a Shooting Match they were introduced to Malcolm Cooper, who twice became the Olympic Gold Medallist in Three Positional Rifle Shooting, and also the World 300m Shooting Record Holder. A record that has never been broken to this day.

Over the next few months an event occurred that really changed the face of sniping for the British Armed Forces. Malcolm Cooper was approached by the Army and asked to make a sniper rifle along the lines of his own rifle, but with the addition of a 10 shot magazine. His own Target Rifle had in fact been built for him by Dave Walls and Dave Caig. The trio got together and produced a rifle that after many trials and a few modifications was accepted for service into the British Armed Forces. It had all the traits of a target rifle but was robust and effective.

The much loved L96 in Combat

During this time most rifle actions were made from round bars of steel. Due to the limited resources of steel available to Walls and Caig, they opted for a rectangular billet of steel to make the action body. This unlikely choice of shape actually gave a number of advantages, not originally noticed from the onset of the action design. The first of these was that you could put four action screws onto the flat surface and you could pull it down evenly onto the other flat surface of the chassis with a resin bond. The flat action body also accommodated a ten shot double row magazine which allowed for fast magazine reloading from the top. The square action also allowed for the fitment of a full length sniper rail along the top. So altogether the result was a robust solid platform that would withstand all the rigours of perceived operational use.

Finally when coupled with the German Schmidt and Bender Scope the rifle exceeded expectations and the single shot killing ability went from 600 to 1000 meters overnight. The rifle was immediately loved by all who used it and this would remain so for the next 25 years until it was finally withdrawn from service. Later the same successful partnership would produce the first effective .338 calibre rifle and their British company, Accuracy International would become the standard setter within the Sniper Rifle World.

TODAY

Today's sniper is armed with the powerful L115A3, the third variant of the combat proven .338 calibre rifle. Armed with the more powerful and variable x25 power Schmidt and Bender Scope the snipers are outshooting their enemy by at least twice the distance. The current longest Recorded Sniper Kill was made by Corporal

L115A3 (.338 calibre) sniper rifle.

of Horse Craig Harrison with this rifle against the Taleban in Afghanistan at a range of 2475 metres.

The shot had an approximate time of flight of around 6 seconds and was estimated to be travelling around 250 metres per second (mps) when it stuck its target.

So not only can the snipers of today shoot further but they can see further too. Armed with an array of the latest optics and equipment the sniper pair is a battle winning combination. Not only can they find the enemy, they can fix them with precision fire thus neutralising the threat.

In this way with the application of the **"Sniper Umbrella"** they can provide cover and support to friendly forces by killing enemy snipers and disrupting enemy attacks by destroying his command and control ability. With the advent of the expected withdraw of combat troops out of Afghanistan in 2013 the sniper will no doubt be looking to take a pace back to the traditional sniper role, of stealth and of stalking. The very ones which were learnt not so long ago in 1916 and of those skills that are as relevant today as it was then.

FUTURE WEAPONS – TODAY

The latest rifles are based upon the combat proven design that has been in service for around 30 years. Coupled with the latest technology and designed to utilitise the latest ammunition design they are the cutting edge of sniping. Accuracy International lead the way with both the AX Series and the Precision Sniper Rifle (PSR.)

The AX series is based upon additional refinement of the L115A3 and the design is available is new a lower profile .338 but .308 (7.62mm) and .50 calibre. The main features are the redesigned chassis, quick adjust butt, cheek piece and rear spike, improved chamber and bolt and the integrated Picatinny rail. The design forces the firer into a new an lower profile which results in a more stable firing platform. This is essential to achieve long range shots. The ability to mount night vision "in line" is achieved by the fore end rail system which allows a number of optics or devices to be mounted to the rifle. One of the key improvements addressed by AX338 is the fitment of a ten round double row magazine, instead of the normal five round version.

A cut away allows the easy removal and replacement of the magazine whilst remaining on the target.

This version of the AX338 is fitted with a 20 inch barrel opposed to the standard 27 inch. The main features of the AX can clearly be seen in this photograph. The rifle scope is the normal in service version Schmidt and Bender 5-25x56 Double Turn.

With developments based upon current combat operations ever evolving the requirement to shoot further continues. The US Military are currently undertaking a project to determine a suitable military sniper rifle under the designation of Precision Sniper Rifle (PSR.) One of the key requirements is that the rifle should be capable of holding 1 MOA at 1500 metres.

Basically that equates to all the shots landing within an area of 450mm. This equates to the width of the average man. One of the other key components is that the rifle must be multi calibre.

In simple terms it must be able to be changed from one calibre to another without additional tools and within minutes.

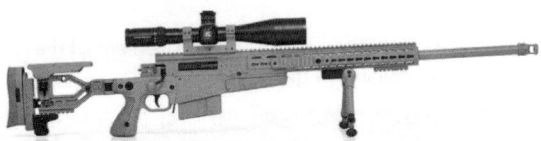

Accuracy International Multi Calibre Precision Sniper Rifle (PSR)

CH 2
COMMAND, ORGANISATION TASKS AND ROLE

BACKGROUND

The sniper platoon forms part of the ISTAR group, which consists of multi-skilled soldiers combining reconnaissance and targeting skills. They may operate as role specific teams or form groups in order to mix capabilities, e.g. sniper pair, recce team and MFC.

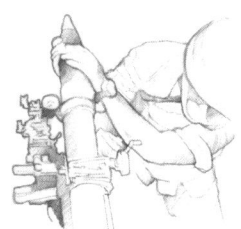

Snipers play an important part in the ISTAR group as through their training and issued equipment, they have both information gathering and targeting capabilities.

ROLE AND TASK

The role of the sniper is to: *"Locate, observe and destroy key enemy personnel and equipment with direct or indirect fire."*

PLATOON COMMANDER

The platoon commander (typically a Senior NCO or C/SGT) advises the chain of command on all matters in relation to sniping.

He commands and conducts sniper platoon level operations and plans and coordinates sniper platoon training. Along with the platoon second-in-command he is responsible for the administration of the sniper platoon.

PLATOON 2IC

Normally a SGT, the platoon 2ic is responsible for the administration of the sniper platoon. He attends the sniper platoon commanders course so he can take on the role of the platoon commander should the platoon commander be disjointed from the platoon.

This dual role aids the continuity of command as the platoon 2ic gains experience and is able to progress on to undertaking the role of platoon commander.

SECTION COMMANDER

The section Commander commands and conducts sniper section operations. He is responsible for the sniper training under guidance from the platoon commander. He is also responsible for the sniper section administration in conjunction with the platoon sergeant and section 2ic.

SNIPER (No1)

The sniper number one is equipped with the L115A3 and engages targets designated by the number two. He should be capable of achieving a first round hit at 900m and providing harassing fire up to 1500m.

SNIPER (No2)

The number two normally controls the sniper pair, he prioritises the targets and provides the firing solutions for the number one. He is responsible for the close protection of the team and also must be in a position to engage opportunity targets at less than the optimum range of the L115A3. The number two is the link to the chain of command and as such is often senior in rank to the number one.

TASKS

Snipers have the following tasks in all operations:
- Disrupt enemy command and control by engaging selected enemy targets with either direct or indirect fire
- Neutralise the enemy by preventing movement and use of weapons by using either direct or indirect fire
- Conduct surveillance from observation posts or temporary positions in order to gather and report timely and accurate information
- Control indirect fire in support of a wider offensive support (OS) template or fire plan
- Neutralise enemy snipers by advising on countersniper measures and by conducting countersniper tasks/ operations

PRINCIPLES OF EMPLOYMENT:
The following principles must be observed when employing snipers

Grouping: The minimum grouping should be a sniper pair and they will operate where they can provide and be provided with mutual support. This mutual support can be provided by other snipers or from manoeuvre sub units.

To ensure that snipers have mutual support a six-man sniper section consisting of three pairs are favoured.

Endurance: As a planning figure, a sniper pair should be able to provide observation with an ability to deliver a precision strike onto a target for 48 hours without resupply. A number of factors can affect this:
- Weather conditions
- Manning and the physical degradation of the sniper pair
- G4 considerations including bowman battery management, water consumption etc.

Co-ordination: The ISTAR officer is responsible for the co-ordination of all patrolling activities within the BG area of operations. This will reduce risk of fratricide and prevent duplication of effort.

The sniper section commander on the ground will command and coordinate the deployed pairs. Each sniper section commander must have an understanding of a higher commander's intent in order to exercise mission command.

> **WHAT IS ISTAR?**
> ISTAR stands for **I**ntelligence, **S**urveillance, **T**arget **A**cquisition, and **R**econnaissance. It links battlefield assets together, from the soldier at street level reporting up, to unmanned drones reporting down, to assist a combat force in employing its sensors and managing the information they gather.
>
> Information (the ground, atmospherics, enemy dispositions and intents) is collected on the battlefield by deployed soldiers as well as a variety of electronic sensors and base cameras.
>
> That information is passed to intelligence personnel for analysis, it then becomes Intelligence which made available to the commander to improve his situational awareness and decision making.

As a direct fire asset, snipers must be integrated into the fire plan in all operations to ensure:
- Correct Briefing
- All activities are co-ordinated
- Suitable tasks are allocated

On occasion the sniper group may be the only asset that can positively identify and engage the target in poor weather conditions.

Tasks: Commanders must be aware of the capabilities of snipers and ensure that they are appropriately tasked on missions that maximise the sniper's effectiveness and survivability.

Command, Organisation Task and Role

Equipment	Description
L115A3	**A** Can achieve a first round hit out to 900 m and harassing fire out to 1500 m. Fitted with a x5 - x25 with variable sight. 8.59 mm. Five round magazine. Can be fitted with a Simrad II and STIC thermal sight. Suppressor can be fitted. Scope for AP ammunition which can penetrate lightly armoured vehicles.
L115A3 L1A1 Leupold Telescope	X12-x40 variable sight. The higher magnification of the telescope allows observation and target detection when the conditions would otherwise prevent it.
PLRF-15C Laser Range Finders	**B** Measure distances from 5M-3000M. Houses a magnetic compass capable of displaying grid or magnetic bearings in mils or degrees to an accuracy of ± 10 mils. It has an inclinometer capable of displaying vertical angles up to an accuracy of ± 3mils. The maximum angle for measurement is ± 800 mils.
KN203 Night Sight (Simrad)	**C** Can aid engagement of targets up to 400m + dependent on ambient light and whether operating in an urban or rural environment.
STIC Sight	Thermal sight that can aid engagement of targets up to 400m+ dependent on temperature, time of day and whether operating in an urban or rural environment. Due to being a thermal sight it is very difficult to positively identify targets at greater ranges.
Kestrel 3000 Pocket Weather Reader	**D** This instrument measures the following environmental conditions: **a.** Wind speed. **b.** Wind chill. **c.** Maximum wind gusts, **d.** Average wind speed, **e.** Temperature, **f.** Relative humidity, **g.** Heat stress, **h.** Dew point.
Advanced Small Arms Targeting Systems (ASATS)	ASATS is a library of ballistic data charts, which provide data for .338 Lapua Magnum and are available for most environmental conditions. These provide the sniper with accurate information to improve the likelihood of a first round hit. The charts quantify: **a.** The bullet drop, **b.** Wind deflection, **c.** Moving target leads

Command, Organisation Task and Role

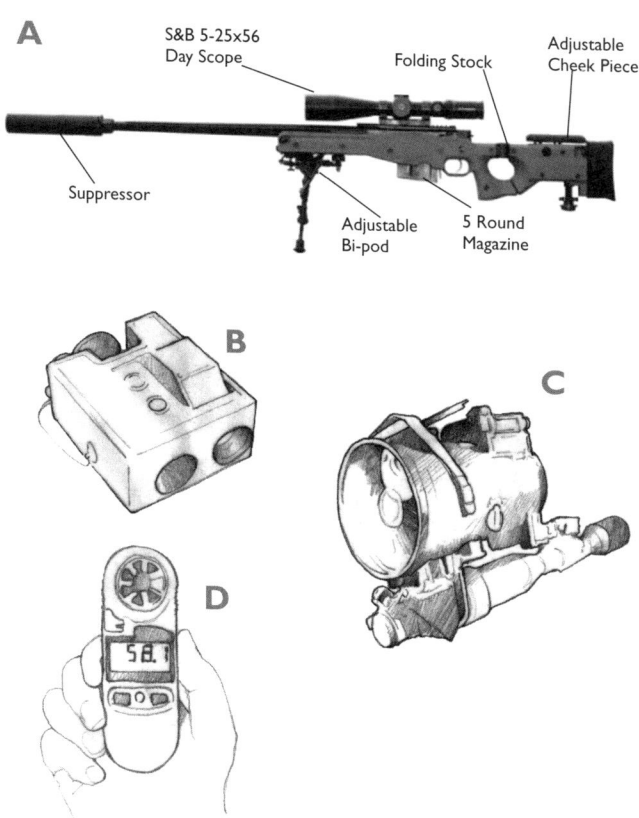

Misc: all weapon ranges given are basic distances and can be increased or decreased dependent on the skill of a sniper and environmental conditions.

Mobility: Snipers need to be able to be deployed quickly if they are to be effectively utilised. If given mobility platforms snipers can quickly deploy to support key phases and points in a battle.

Sniper teams can be deployed by a variety of different vehicles

The sniper platoon is not currently scaled for any vehicles so reallocation of resources or careful task organisation needs to be conducted.

The most suitable from of transport on operations for the snipers would be the a quad bike and trailer, ideally two in each platoon.

USES IN PHASES OF WAR
Snipers can be employed on the following tasks during the following phases of war:
- Offensive Operations
- Defensive Operations
- Delay Operations
- Traditional Phases During Operations
- Stability Operations
- Counter Sniping Operations

TRAINING

THE SEVEN SNIPER SKILLS
Specialist training for snipers is generally listed as "The Seven Sniper Skills." These are illustrated as steps, each one leading to the next. Every skill and step is important, for example unless preparation and map study in selection of the route is done well, the sniper may not reach his objective to use his others skills.

All the skills are important and the sniper must master each one of them. Training is carried out at both unit level and at one of the numerous training establishments. The typical course lasts around nine weeks and to pass each skill a score of at least 70% is required. For the marksmanship the pass rate is increased to 80%. The size of the course could vary but is normally made up of 16 students. Those deemed successful are "badged" with the much sought after sniper qualification badge.

Stalking

Concealment

Observation

Shooting

Judging Distance

Navigation

Sniper Knowledge

SNIPER MARKSMANSHIP

Shooting and Marksmanship are the Sniper's *9-5 bread and butter* disciplines, to readers who have done some shooting before and thought that Position and Hold etc.. was all there was too it prepare yourself for a read that if nothing else will convince you that snipers are not just squaddies with long barreled weapons but are truly the "hunters" of the battlefield.

Below are some terms explained that you will come across in the following pages and a picture detailing the target dimensions.

MPI –   Mean Point of Impact (The centre of the group)
POA -   Point Of Aim
POI -   Point Of Impact
CZP -   Correct Zero Point – Where the rounds should land when zeroing.
ESA -   Estimated/Expected Scoring Area
MOA   Minute of Angle – A measurement of 1/60 of a degree. Each MOA is equivalent to 25mm per 100 yards or 30mm per 100m. The 7.62mm and .338 Rifles would normaly shoot a group of 1 MOA. For .50 Calibres this would be closer to 2 MOA

MIL RAD   The 5x25 56mm Power Variable Schmitt and Bender Sight is calibrated at 1 click at 100m = 10mm

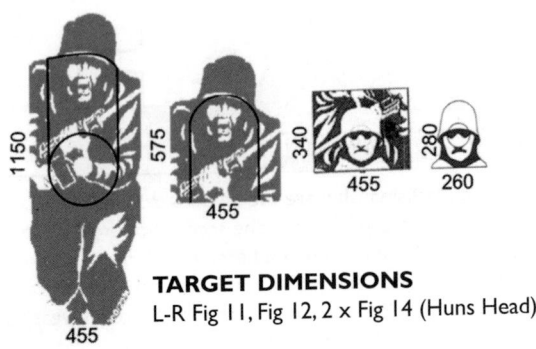

TARGET DIMENSIONS
L-R Fig 11, Fig 12, 2 x Fig 14 (Huns Head)

INTERNAL BALLISTICS

THE BULLET
The bullet is made up of two different metals (see picture - page 3-3) the jacket is made of a copper alloy wrapped around a lead core. Remember that the bullet is larger than the barrel and consequently the design allows it to be squeezed into the grooves of the rifling and forced up the bore. For The .338 (8.59mm) the standard in service military bullet weighs 252 grains and gives the best compromise allowing velocity, range and penetration.

THE CASE
The brass case holds the parts of the round together and is flexible enough to expand and thus form a gas tight seal in the chamber.

THE PRIMER
The primer consists of a small pressed metal cap which contains an explosive compound that when struck ignites the propellant.

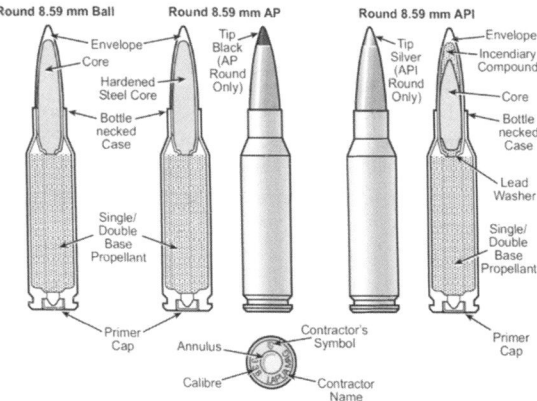

THE BARREL

The barrel of the sniper rifle is free floating, which means that it is only in contact with the action body at the chamber. The normal .338 27 inch barrel has 4 grooves that twist to the right with a 1 in 11 pitch. This simply means that there is one full twist for every eleven inches or 280mm.

RIFLE BARREL - NAMED PARTS

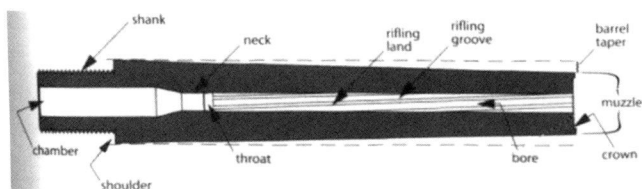

FIRING ACTION

The sequence is as follows:
a. Firing pin strikes the primer.
b. Primer ignites the propellant.
c. Propellant burns and rapidly increases the gas pressure.
d. Increased pressure forces the bullet out into the barrel
e. Bullet enters the rifling which imparts spin and it leaves the barrel at around 840-870 metres per second, this is also known as muzzle velocity.

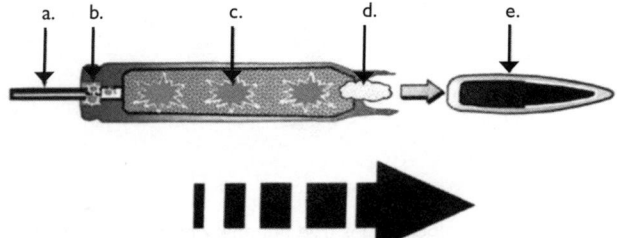

EFFECT OF INCREASED CHAMBER PRESSURES

The effect of increased chamber pressure leads to a higher muzzle velocity which in turn causes the round to strike high of the target. Common causes are oil and water found in both the chamber and on the bullet case.

At its worse this excessive pressure could cause an explosion or bulging in the barrel. Care must be taken to remove all water and oil from the ammunition and chamber prior to live firing. Excessive fouling and bullet debris can also cause high chamber pressures. In hot environments the increased temperature of both the ammunition and chamber can also cause high pressures, resulting in shots going high and hard extractions.

HARMONICS

Barrel Harmonics is simply the vibration of the barrel caused by the bullet moving up the bore once fired. The barrel moves in a whip like motion from the chamber to the muzzle. The bullet will always leave the barrel at the point of most vibration. To be accurate all the rounds fired must leave the barrel at the same point of vibration. Therefore it is important not to interfere with the harmonics by resting the barrel or by putting too much scrim on the barrel itself. The barrel must retain its free floating action at all times.

JUMP ANGLE

This is simply the amount of movement that the barrel makes from the time of the shot to the recoil. If the jump angle is restricted the harmonics are not correct and the shot will miss.

THE 'COLD BORE' SHOT

A 'Cold Bore' shot is the first shot fired after the bore has been cleaned or after the rifle has been stored dirty for an extended period of time.

The sniper must be able to predict where his cold bore shot is going to go as more than likely this will be the most important round he fires. At times the first two rounds can both deviate from the remainder.

The average deviation appears to be 2-3cm at 100m. A typical example can be seen on the right:
In this case the rifle was taken from the armoury and was not dry patched prior to live firing. The small amount of oil/solvent left in the barrel has caused the first shot to land higher than the subsequent four.

Snipers need to practise and record separate data for the first round shots. Consideration should be made to recording the average displacement for these shots as an adjustment could be required to the scope settings when firing Cold Bore Shots.

EXTERNAL BALLISTICS
This is the effect on the bullet once it has left the barrel. The bullet is at its fastest when it is approximately 100m from the muzzle. The speed of the bullet reduces due to air resistance impeding its flight. In turn the effect of gravity causes the bullet to be pulled downwards toward the earth.

CULMINATION POINT
The highest point reached by the round on its trajectory to the target is called the Culmination Point (CP). It is approximately 2/3rds of the way to the target. Consideration much be given with regards to shooting over certain cover or under an obstruction.

To better illustrate this, there was a recent case of a Police Marksman in the US who hit and killed a bystander who was standing on a footbridge midway between the shooter and above the target.

MARKSMANSHIP PRINCIPLES

ARC OF BULLET TRAJECTORY

Bullet Flight – Trajectory to Target

Line of Sight Axis

Culmination Point

PRINCIPLES OF GOOD SHOOTING:
- The position and hold must be firm enough to support the weapon.
- The weapon must point naturally at the target without any undue physical effort.
- Sight alignment and the sight picture must be correct.
- The shot must be released and followed through without any undue disturbance to the position.

ELEMENTS OF A GOOD SHOOTING POSITION:

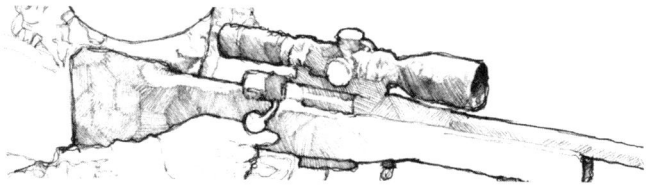

- Muscular relaxation
- Bone support
- Natural alignment onto POA

FACTORS COMMON TO ALL GOOD FIRING POSITIONS:
- Left-hand, elbow and legs.
- The position of the butt
- Right hand/trigger handgrip
- Right elbow
- Spot weld
- Relaxation
- Breathing

FACTORS AFFECTING APPLICATION OF FIRE:
- **F** - firing position
- **L** - light
- **A** - attachments
- **P** - positional support
- **W** - wind
- **I** - inefficient zero
- **W** - wet and oily ammo or chamber

APPLICATION OF FIRE
This simply means applying your shots onto the area of the target you want to hit.

ATTACHMENTS
As the barrel of the sniper rifle has a free floating action any attachment will alter the harmonics and also the jump angle. This will therefore alter the shot.

ANGLE
Whether shooting from an upwards or downwards angle the shot will always hit high. This amount of error will be the same for both upwards and downwards angular shooting due to the gravity pull (See Angle Shooting)

FIRE POSITIONS
A change in the fire position from which the weapon was zeroed will result in a change of position of the MPI. Building a good position will reduce the displacement. For subsequent shoots the firer should try to shoot each one exactly the same without disturbing his position.

With training the sniper can fire, follow through and manipulate the bolt whilst maintaining his sight picture, thus ready to continue the engagement if needed. This practice also gives the sniper a chance to remain unseen throughout the shot as his actions are very slow and slight, thereby limiting movement that could be seen by the enemy.

IN EFFICIENT ZERO

If a good zero is not achieved then that error multiplies the further you get from the target. The sniper must ensure that his centre of point of impact (POA) on the target matches the centre of his correct aiming point (CZP)

This is often best achieved by measuring the group size with a ruler and finding the correct centre point. The three round group is often used to check zero the sniper rifle.

LIGHT

Light affects how the individual perceives the image of the target. In bright light the target will be clearer therefore making the target seem closer. With a clearer image the fire will tend to be lower and in poor light higher. The rule is "lights up sights up."

MUZZLE BREAK

The muzzle break serves two purposes. Firstly it can act as a flash eliminator and secondly it controls and reduces the jump angle therefore allowing the sniper to still be able to see his shot on the target during the recoil.

muzzle break

The muzzle break can also act as the fixture where upon a tactical suppressor can be fitted, thereby reducing the muzzle signature further.

PARALLEL ERROR

Parallel error is simply the error made whilst aiming at the target resulting in subsequent shots printing on the target in the direction of the error. If you are aiming slightly off centre when you fire the result on the target will be the same.

POSITIONAL SUPPORT

The resting of a weapon on any part of your body will result in displacement of the MPI. The type of ground you are firing from can also affect the jump angle, i.e. a hard surface.

Care should be taken not to force the rifle into a shooting position but to allow it to recoil naturally. Never rest the barrel against anything.

In the picture you'll notice how the rifle is placed on top of the sand bag and is allowed to rest without pressure placed upon it by the firer. The rifle will recoil a few centimetres rearwards whilst the improvised tripod will remain still, pushed into the ground. The firer's left hand is acting only as a support and does not influence the rifle of position.

WIND

Wind is the biggest factor that will move the MPI. *It is also the biggest cause of missing the target.*

As the wind constantly changes in both direction and strength skill is needed to carefully predict what the wind is doing. Accurate wind reading is essential to hitting targets at range within a couple of shots.

Although you do get some vertical lift on certain types of ammunition, the majority of shots land at the correct elevation however they may miss both left and right dependent upon the wind conditions.

The wind closest to the barrel has the biggest influence on the bullet's flight, which is why the most valuable reading of the wind is the one taken at the firers position.

POSITIONAL TESTING AND ADJUSTING

The key to shooting accurately at long distance is to practice by dry firing, testing and adjusting before live firing. Modern sniper rifle designs allow and force the shooter into the most stable firing positions.

The key factor is to have the rifle supporting its own weight without human influence. This can be achieved by use of the bipod and a rice sock or sandbag. The rifle is naturally aligned onto the target and then the firer takes up a suitable position concentrating on squeezing the trigger without affecting the rifle.

THE SEQUENCE OF TEST AND ADJUSTING

The build-up of a preferred firing position involves:
- Relaxing - this is also often called getting into the sniper bubble.
- Confirming you have the correct sight picture and the sight alignment is correct.
- Ensuring the rifle is not cantered and is square to the target.
- Take control of the trigger and have the confidence to feel and control it by gentle squeezing short of the first stage. This can

also be achieved when the safety catch is applied however a more seasoned sniper should do this with the safety catch set to fire.
- Start your breathing cycle and complete at least two cycles with your eyes closed.
- Open your eyes and observe your sight picture.
- If you are not happy break the position and rebuild from scratch.
- Continue the whole test and adjust process until you are happy the rifle naturally points at the target without any physical effort.

TYPES OF TRIGGER CONTROL

There are two types:
- Interrupted
- Uninterrupted

Interrupted simply means that the firer takes the trigger to the first pressure, pauses and then squeezes the trigger to the second stage, firing the shot. Uninterrupted means that the whole sequence occurs by squeezing from first to second stage without pause.

The type of trigger control is down to personal choice, based upon experience of shooting.

FACTORS THAT DETERMINE GOOD TRIGGER CONTROL:
- A good shooting hand grip on the rifle
- Correct trigger finger placement.

The trigger should be operated smoothly by squeezing the trigger. This can be done by holding up the first stage and squeezing through the second or by squeezing the trigger continuously through to the second stage. Common errors in trigger control include flinching, snatching and jerking the trigger back.

Trigger finger placement is a matter of personal preference again based upon shooting experience, some favour the full finger position while others just the tip resting on the trigger.

Trigger pull from correct placement of the finger on the trigger up to the First Stage (Pressure)

Squeezing through from First Stage to the Second Stage (Firing)

REMEMBER:
SMOOTH, POSITIVE, AUTOMATIC
DIRECT TO THE REAR

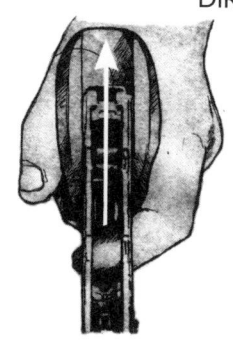
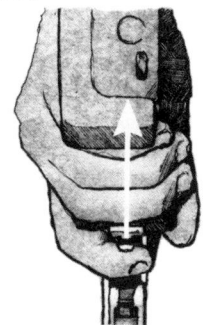

There is no doubt that the key to long range accurate shooting is to have a firm fully supported position and smooth trigger pull.

THE RIFLE SCOPE

*Schmidt & Bender
5-25x56 PMII*

INTRODUCTION
The in service sniper rifle – L115A3 comes fitted with the PMII telescopic Scope, the standard issued being the 5-25 x56 with Mildot. This scope gives additional advantage to the user by way of an observation aid allowing individuals to be identified (PID) prior to any engagement.

SCHMIDT & BENDER 5-25 X 56 PMII

CHARACTERISTICS
The Elevation and Deflection Drums are graduated in increments of 0.1 Mil Rad, this equates to each click adjustment being 10mm at

100 metres. The elevation drum has a Double Turn adjustment thus giving target engagement, once zeroed at 100 metres out to around 2000 metres. There are 260 clicks of elevation, 140 on the bottom scale and 120 on the upper (coloured yellow.) The deflection drum has 60 clicks of adjustment both left and right.

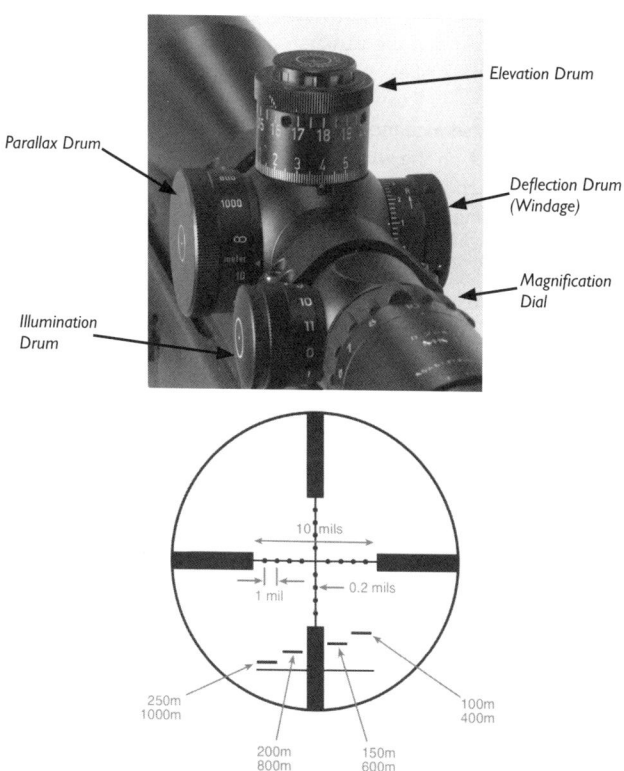

SCHMIDT & BENDER 3-12 X 50 PMII

INTRODUCTION
The 3-12x50 riflescope is a combat proven optical device that has been in service since the early 90's. It was fitted to the L96A1 and the earlier .338 L115A1 and A2 rifles.

A number are in service mounted on the AW50 but on the whole it is generally underpowered for both .338 and .50 having only a single turn of elevation.

The scope is matched perfectly to the 7.62mm round and as such is suitable for mounting on some in service semi automatic sniper rifles such as the Heckler and Koch 417 and some versions of the L129A1 Sharp Shooter Rifle.

This scope has 130 clicks of elevation and 130 (65 left and 65 right) of deflection.

CORRECT SIGHT ALIGNMENT

Points to check are:
- Eye relief
- Ocular lens
- Objective lens
- Target

Sight picture

- Fully focused on the mil dot reticle
- No scope shadow
- Mil dot horizontally and vertically placed in the sight picture.

 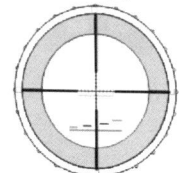 

- If the distance eye - eyepiece is good, then the whole of the reticle and the full field of view will be visible.
- If the distance eye - eyepiece is too short, then a shadow will appear at the extreme edges of the reticle, and the field of view will be narrower.
- If the distance eye - eyepiece is too long, then the extreme edges of the reticle are not visible, and the field of view will be narrower.

ANGULAR SHIFT ERROR

This error is common when using typical battle sights such as the issued emergency ones or when using the pistol. Snipers need to know this as the conditions when you will use these sights means that the target will be at a closer range.

The normal correct sight picture is like this. The front and rear notches are lined up equally and square. This is now aimed at the centre of mass on the target

Failure to get this right gives angular shift error and the bullet displaces based upon the error. Here are some typical examples. The shot placement ● is shown on the target and corresponds to the error:

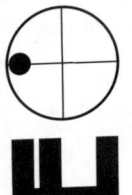   

OTHER CONDITIONS THAT COULD AFFECT THE SHOT
- Temperature
- Humidity
- Rain
- Clothing.

WINDAGE
Factors affecting the determination of wind:
- Strength of the wind
- Direction of the wind
- Range to the target.

STRENGTH OF THE WIND
Determining wind strength or velocity is the first step in calculating how much a bullet may be deflected. There are 5 recognised wind strengths. They are:

Strength	mph	kph
Gentle	5	8
Moderate	10	16
Fresh	15	24
Strong	20	32
Very Strong	25+	40

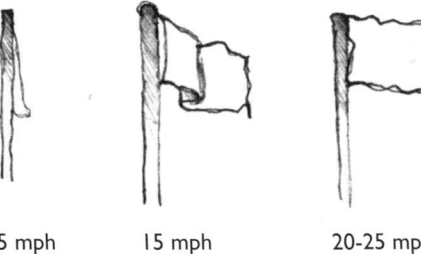

5 mph
8 kph

15 mph
24 kph

20-25 mph
32-40 kph

Sniper Marksmanship

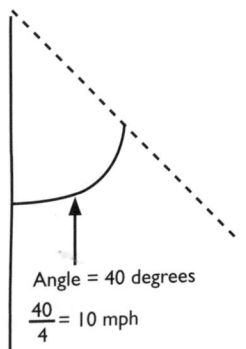

Angle = 40 degrees

$\frac{40}{4}$ = 10 mph

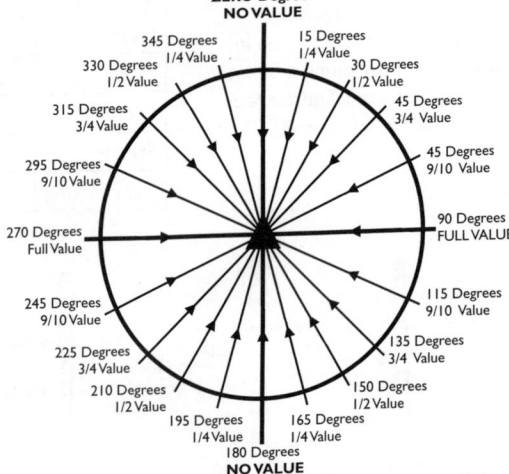

DIRECTION OF THE WIND (WIND VALUE)

POINTING METHOD

Drop some grass and observe the angle at which it falls and then divide by four.

The method can also be used to determine wind speed from flags. The technique is the same. The angle of the flag divided by 4 = Wind Speed

MIRAGE

Mirage, when present, is an excellent aid to judging wind velocity up to approximately 20 kph. It can be seen all the way down the range and is enhanced with the use of binos or spotting scope.

Some mirage patterns are:

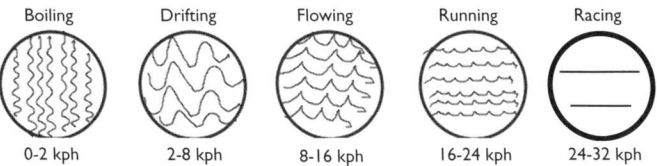

Boiling	Drifting	Flowing	Running	Racing
0-2 kph	2-8 kph	8-16 kph	16-24 kph	24-32 kph

DISTANCE TO THE TARGET

Knowing the distance to the target is important when making bullet deflection calculations. The further the distance the longer the bullet is in the air. This gives more time for the wind to deflect the bullet. The bullet takes approximately 1 second to fly 600m and nearly 2 seconds to reach 1000m.

METHODS OF DETERMINING WIND DIRECTION

- Flags method
- Wind direction indicators
- Observation method
- Pointing method
- Mirage

- Sight, feel, sense, calibration
- SWAG (Scientific Wild Arse Guess!)

Sequence.
- Range to target
- Wind Strength
- Wind Direction
- Sight Adjustment

SOURCES OF ERROR IN SHOOTING

RIFLE:
Loose scope mount screws: The scope mount must be secured to the sight bracket.

Trigger: The trigger should have a smooth two-stage action. Although fully adjustable the standard L115A3 trigger is set at 1.8 kg pressure.

Butt adjustment: This must be correct to the firer to ensure the correct eye relief.

Barrel jump interference: Errors caused by the rifle are usually connected with some interference with the jump angle. Typical examples are:
- Dirty/fouled barrel
- Oil in the barrel
- Oil in the chamber
- Damaged barrel
- Resting the barrel
- Hot chamber/barrel
- Loose butt pad

AMMUNITION:

A number of causes of bad shooting are caused by ammunition issues. Typical examples are:
- Oily or wet ammunition
- Dirt caused by sand or snow
- Hot ammunition, caused by exposure to the sun
- Mixed batches
- Mixed natures of ammunition i.e.: ball and tracer in one magazine.
- Tracer. (The tracer element is corrosive and will cause damage to the barrel if it is not cleaned out, although you should not be concerned about using them)
- Sighting shot by tracer: The tracer element burns at different rates therefore you would expect the ball ammunition to strike the target differently to the tracer round. The tracer effect is only a guide as to where the shot has gone

POOR SHOOTING

In the event of a poor shot occurring for no apparent reason, the sniper must think and check logically that all relevant conditions have been allowed for. If this does not reveal the source of the error then he must check his equipment and in particular the following:
- Correct Sight Setting
- Sight is securely mounted
- Elevation and deflection drums are secure and tight
- The sight is level and not cantered
- Bipod fitted correctly and not loose
- Muzzle break is secure
- Tactical suppressor, if fitted, is tight and not damaged
- Check the rifle is clean

MISS DRILL

If you are missing the target you should attempt to fire somewhere where you will be able to see your fall of shot. Normally a mound, clear piece of ground or a hard target will allow you to observe the strike and splash of the shot. Sometimes you may have to walk your shot onto the target using this method. Other methods that can help you include:

- **Swirl:**
  This is the round disturbing the air during flight giving a good indication of the fall of shot

- **Strike/Splash:**
  The Sniper No 2 should be employed to pick up the Strike/Splash as he is not affected by the recoil and has better optics

- **Tracer:**
  Can be employed, but is a double-edged weapon as it will give your position away. It will give you an indication of the wind and the fall of shot remembering the limitations though of the tracer ammunition. IR tracer is available and could be used in the dark without fear of giving the snipers location away

The Spotters View:
The swirl flight path can be seen as the bullet falls onto the target from the top right corner. Commonly the area arrowed is where you will see the swirl pattern.

The swirl is often picked up at the midway point to the target. The spotter should focus at the mid way point which is half way to the target.

The **white arrow line** is the snipers sight picture view.

ALTERNATIVE SHOOTING POSITIONS

Improvised Tripod – Kneeling Position

Improvised Tripod – Kneeling Position

SLING SUPPORTED

Kneeling Position – using the sling to support the rifle.

The sling is fitted like so. This is called the "Two Point Sling."

Sniper Marksmanship

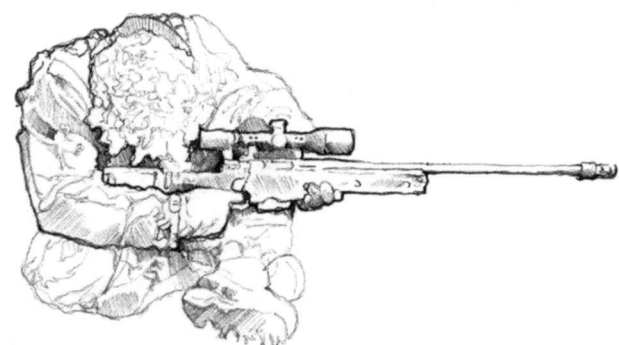

An alternative stable sitting position. One for the more flexible!

Conventional Sitting Position. Feet can be crossed or relaxed. Elbows are resting on the knees, but not directly. Knee and elbow pads must be used in between.

HAWKINS POSITION

Left hand forward acting as an improvised rest. The butt of the rifle rests or is forced into the ground.

HAWKINS SLING

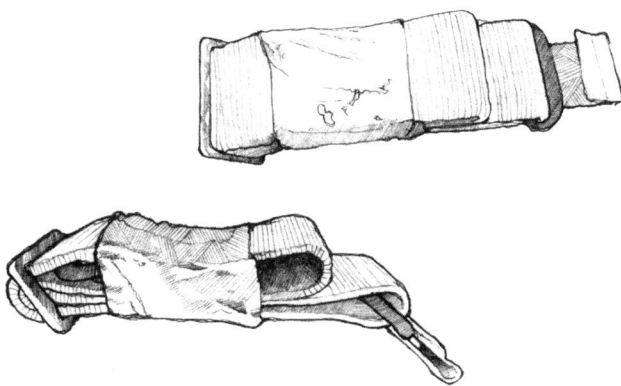

Using the smaller part of the sling the webbing is taped up like so acting as a firm support to the rifle when grasped.

GROUPING AND ZEROING

DEFINITION OF A GROUP
A series of shots, not less than three, fired from the same rifle at the same point of aim will seldom, if ever, pass through the same hole but will produce a pattern on the target. This pattern is known as a group.

A good 5 Round Group

THEORY OF A GROUP
The size of the group will grow in direct proportion to the range.

Remember 30mm equates to 1 MOA so therefore 1 MOA at 300m would give an ESA of around 90mm.

The spread and pattern that appears can also be used to determine errors that have been made in the shooting.

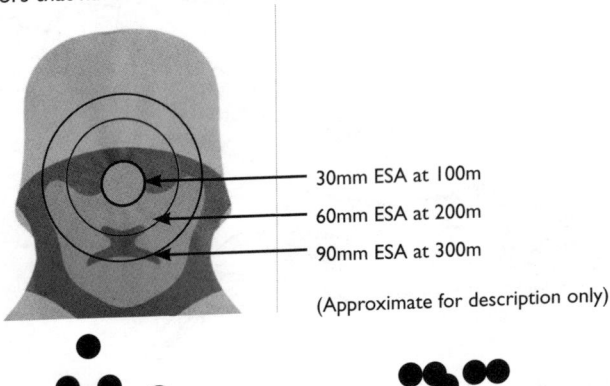

- 30mm ESA at 100m
- 60mm ESA at 200m
- 90mm ESA at 300m

(Approximate for description only)

Pulled Shot off the group

Trigger Control-not smooth

GROUPING AND ZEROING THE RIFLE AND SCOPE

SIMPLE TARGET ADJUSTMENT - RANGE 100 METRES.

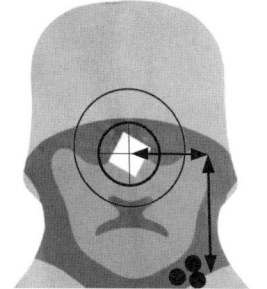

To adjust the three round group find the centre of mass for the group fired. Then measure the height in mm to the Correct Zeroing Point (CZP) Then adjust the deflection left or right to the same point.

Three Round Group Adjustment

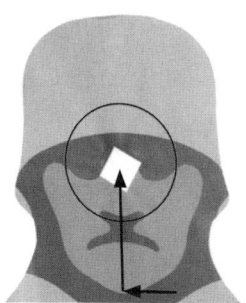

In this case the adjustments were 120mm up and 30mm left. As each click = 10mm the adjustments to the scope would be:

12 clicks up
3 clicks left.

A check zero group is then re-shot.

As long as the group falls exactly at the CZP then the rifle is zeroed.

The scope drums are loosened and taking care not to move them are re set to 0 (Zero) Elevation and 0 (Zero) Deflection.

If required a further confirmation check group can be shot to confirm the new rifle zero.

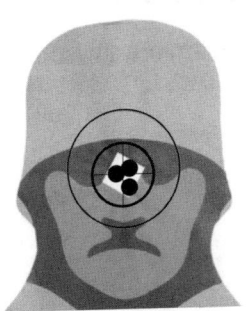

FIELD QUICK ADJUSTMENT/CHECK ZERO

A quick method of adjustment in the field is to move the cross hairs to the fall of shot and then by re aiming at the original POA the error is quickly adjusted without having to call the adjustment in clicks/mils. It works like this:

1. First shot (White Arrow) Blown off the target by wind. Elevation is correct.

2. Then by holding the rifle still, the sight deflection drum is turned to the Point of Impact (POI) in the direction of the bottom arrow, thus moving the cross hairs onto the error. A vertical adjustment can also be made at this stage if required.

3. The rifle is then aimed at the target using the centre of mass POA as before with the first shot. The target is engaged and hit centrally.

QUICK TARGET ADJUSTMENT

So to recap the idea is to quickly adjust the fall of shot onto the target as easily as possible. This simple method can be quicker than the standard military method of making adjustments based upon the range and the value of each click accordingly.

This method is very effective when determining correct elevation. The biggest problem as mentioned is due to the effect of wind however this can be easily overcome using patient wind calling and experience.

For training it is suggested to fire two shots before making such adjustments, thereby giving you a group that can be accurately adjusted.

In the future, snipers will use the reticule pattern to make adjustments, in the same way as the "Hold System" is used.

For helicopter sniping holds are the quickest method due to the unstable platform and time constraints. The scope is turned down to the minimum magnification. The most effective method is to use a Semi Automatic Rifle in this role.

MOVING TARGET ENGAGEMENT
Factors effecting engaging moving targets:
- Range to target
- Wind
- Direction the target is moving
- Speed of the target

RANGE TO TARGET
- As the range increases out to a moving target so will the lead, as long as the target moves at the same speed

WIND CONSIDERATION
- Once the target range has been established the wind correction adjustment needs applying to the scope before any alteration for a moving target

DIRECTION THE TARGET IS MOVING
- Crossing at 90° requires FULL LEAD
- Crossing obliquely requires HALF THE LEAD
- Directly towards or away from you needs no lead

SPEED OF THE TARGET
- There are four generic speeds for the average man and two for moving vehicles
- All speeds are approximate and require practice to become competent

Mil Lead for a human target

Speed	Aim Off in Mils (Range)									
	100	200	300	400	500	600	700	800	900	1000
Slow Patrol 1.25 km/h	0	0	0.1	0.1	0.2	0.25	0.3	0.4	0.50	0.50
Fast Patrol 2 km/h	0	0.1	0.2	0.3	0.4	0.4	0.5	0.6	0.7	0.8
Slow Walk 4.25 km/h	0.1	0.3	0.4	0.6	0.7	0.9	1.1	1.3	1.5	1.7
Fast Walk 6 km/h	0.2	0.4	0.6	0.8	1.0	1.3	1.6	1.8	2.2	2.4

Mil Lead for a vehicle target

Speed	Aim Off in Mils (Range)									
	100	200	300	400	500	600	700	800	900	1000
Slow Patrol 1.25 km/h	0.25	0.50	0.8	1.0	1.4	1.7	2.1	2.5	2.9	3.1
Slow Patrol 1.25 km/h	0.50	1.0	1.6	2.2	2.8	3.5	4.2	4.9	5.7	6.25

METHODS OF ENGAGEMENT FOR MOVING TARGETS:
- Dialling on wind corrections
- Ambush method
- Tracking method

DIALLING ON WIND CORRECTION
- Add corrections to scope rather than Ambush or Track Methods.
- Dial the wind and lead corrections onto the scope directly
    E.g. Wind = add 20 right
    Target moving from the right to left requires lead of 4.0 Mil
    Dial 20 R then Dial 40 L
    This gives us 20 L on the scope – crosshairs on the target and engage

Dial 20 R for Wind.

Dial in 40 L for the 4.0 Mil target.

The conclusion is the windage showing 20 L

AMBUSHING METHOD
- Engage the target by placing the lead on a point in front of where the target is travelling. Once the target reaches the lead the shot is fired.

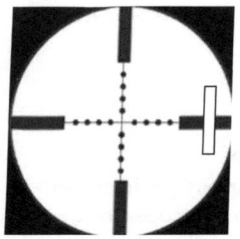

A 4.0 Mil Lead is chosen for a target moving to the left.

Once the target reaches the lead the shot is fired and hits the target within the crosshairs.

TRACKING METHOD
- The lead must be worked out in the same way however the target is tracked by keeping the lead on the moving target.

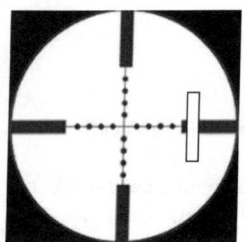

A 2.0 Mil Lead is chosen for a target moving to the left.

Once the target reaches the lead the shot is fired and hits the target within the crosshairs.

CONCLUSIONS:
- Hitting a moving target is difficult and not likely beyond 1000m.
- Be prepared for misses and rapid follow up shots
- Good concise sniper observer dialogue is required
- Experience shows that in combat there is no time for lengthy mathematics equations
- Practice of leads and determination is the key to rapid moving target engagement

ANGLED SHOOTING

REASONS FOR
- There is a physical ballistic problem encountered when shooting on angles that causes the bullets point of impact to hit high
- If the target is up or down on an angle, the sniper must aim low because the bullet will impact high
- When we zero in our rifle at 100 meters, we are shooting on a flat plane with the full force of gravity pushing down on the bullet
- However, when we shoot on an incline or decline (up or down on an angle) the force and effect of gravity is less on the bullet; but the sight height above the bore of the barrel remains the same, or adjusted for shooting on a flat plane
- So to engage targets at angles we need to work out the Flat Line Distance or Gravity Range and dial it in

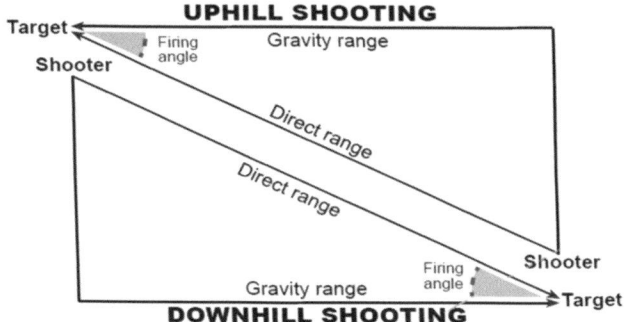

Same rules apply for both downhill and uphill shooting

CONSIDERATIONS
- Range to Target from Firer
- Angle from which taken
- The method to use to work out the cosine
- Capabilities of the weapon being employed

THE COSINE METHOD

Direct Range by Laser 500 metres
Firing Angle Up Hill 30°

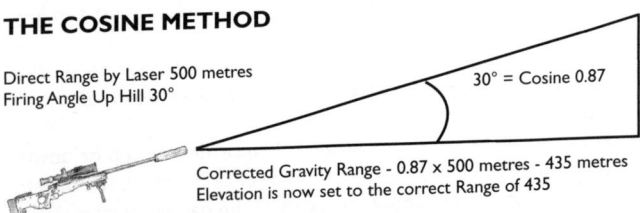

30° = Cosine 0.87

Corrected Gravity Range - 0.87 x 500 metres - 435 metres
Elevation is now set to the correct Range of 435

THE COSINE METHOD FORMULA
- Range to Target from Firer (Sight Line).
- Need to know the angle of the barrel.
- Need to know the cosine for that angle.
- Covert the sum Sight Line Range x Cosine = correct Gravity Distance.
- Apply this correction to the sight.

Sniper Marksmanship

ANGLE	COSINE	ANGLE	COSINE	ANGLE	COSINE
1	1	31	0.857	61	0.484
2	0.999	32	0.848	62	0.469
3	0.998	33	0.838	63	0.453
4	0.997	34	0.829	64	0.438
5	0.996	35	0.819	65	0.422
6	0.994	36	0.809	66	0.406
7	0.992	37	0.798	67	0.390
8	0.990	38	0.788	68	0.374
9	0.987	39	0.777	69	0.358
10	0.984	40	0.766	70	0.342
11	0.981	41	0.754	71	0.325
12	0.978	42	0.743	72	0.309
13	0.974	43	0.731	73	0.292
14	0.970	44	0.719	74	0.275
15	0.965	45	0.707	75	0.258
16	0.961	46	0.694	76	0.241
17	0.956	47	0.681	77	0.224
18	0.951	48	0.669	78	0.207
19	0.945	49	0.656	79	0.190
20	0.939	50	0.642	80	0.173
21	0.933	51	0.629	81	0.156
22	0.927	52	0.615	82	0.139
23	0.920	53	0.601	83	0.121
24	0.913	54	0.587	84	0.104
25	0.906	55	0.573	85	0.087
26	0.898	56	0.559	86	0.069
27	0.891	57	0.544	87	0.052
28	0.882	58	0.529	88	0.034
29	0.874	59	.0515	89	0.017
30	0.866	60	0.5	90	0

THE ANGLE COSINE INDICATOR

The Indicator gives you the cosine angle number from the Cosine Chart.

The cosine 0. number is then used to calculate the sum thus giving the new adjusted Gravity Distance Range setting.

POINTS
- There is no need for adjustment when the target is an angle less than 10°
- There could be some vertical distortion on targets greater than 49° therefore the new sum is:

Range x Cosine x Consign = Gravity Distance
Example: 395m x (49° - cosine) 0.65 x 0.65 = 167m

RIFLE CLEANING

Cleaning protocol is important to not only maintain accuracy of the sniper rifle but also to extend the barrel life. Currently a number of sniper groups around the world are finding problems maintaining accuracy particularly at long range due to incorrectly cleaned rifle barrels.

The correct choice of cleaning solvents coupled with good technique will prolong the accuracy of the rifle. Current thinking suggests chemical cleaning using both copper and carbon removers.

In some cases these cleaning solutions are mixed in one container thus making it easier for the sniper to clean the rifle. Of note is the excessive wear caused when using the .338 calibre rifle such as the L115A3.

Specialist Ammunition
Specialist ammunition such as Tracer and AP/API does have a tendency to induce excessive wear on the barrel however its usage should not be deferred as the target must always dictate what sort of ammunition is to be used.

Cleaning Notes:
Recommended Barrel Life
- Barrel life .338/8.59mm -2500 – 3000 rounds
- Tactical Suppressor life -2500 – 3000 rounds

Recommended Cleaning Cycle
- For 7.62mm - barrel to be pulled through after 100 rounds Ball or 50 rounds AP
- For 8.59mm - barrel to be pulled through after 60 rounds Ball or 40 rounds AP

Cleaning Cycle

The rifle needs regular cleaning. During this the rifle can also be inspected for damage and then lubricated as required or conditions dictate. Other points include:
- The bore should be pulled through until it is dry
- The chamber should be dry cleaned
- Magazines should be inspected to ensure that they are not damaged. Check that no more than 10 rounds or the amount of rounds ordered are loaded into each magazine
- In heavy rain and damp conditions keep the muzzle cover and sight cover fitted for as long as possible. (The rifle can be fired in an emergency with the muzzle cover fitted.)

BARREL CLEANING PROCEDURE

The recommended cleaning procedure is as follows, this is generic to all bolt action rifles. The bore and chamber are easier to clean immediately after firing whilst the barrel is still warm however this may not always be operationally practical.
- Apply solvent to a patch, apply to the bore from the breech end using a cleaning rod guide. Push through once and remove at the muzzle
- Fit the correct size Phosphor Bronze brush and wet with the solvent, pass the brush completely through the bore in each direction several times, repeat with fresh solvent
- Refit the jag to the rod and pass a clean patch through the bore and remove at the muzzle. **DO NOT PULL THE PATCH BACK INTO THE BORE**
- Repeat this operation until the patches come out clean (a light grey smudge is acceptable)

If using a separate copper Solvent then apply copper solvent to a clean patch and wet bore, leave to soak for 5 minutes (or as directed on the bottle) then clean out with a new patch, heavy fouling will show as blue on the patch. Repeat if required, then dry clean.

An example of Carbon and Copper fouling inside the barrel:

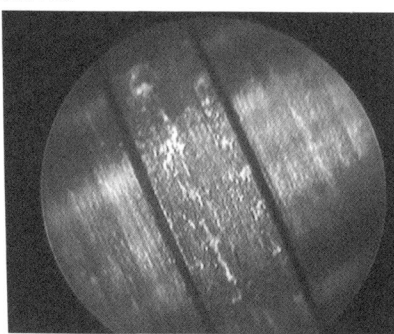

Notice how the shiny copper deposits sit on a layer of "crazy paving" effect carbon.

The aim is to remove both by vigorous cleaning and the correct use of solvent cleaners, to the naked eye the barrel may look polished and clean.

Excessive Wear

Excessive Fouling

The typical barrel will have excessive fouling and wear as shown above. Cleaning should be concentrated on where the excessive fouling occurs as well as the whole length of the barrel.

STANDARD ISSUED CLEANING KIT
Left to Right – anti clockwise:
- Cleaning Rod Guide
- Phosphor Bronze brush and Cleaning Rod
- Chamber Brush
- Jag
- Small dusting brush
- Flannelette Patches (These for 7.62mm and a larger boxed one for the .338.)
- Allen Key Multi tool
- Break free Bore Cleaner and Oil.

* Specialist Copper and Carbon cleaners not shown above.

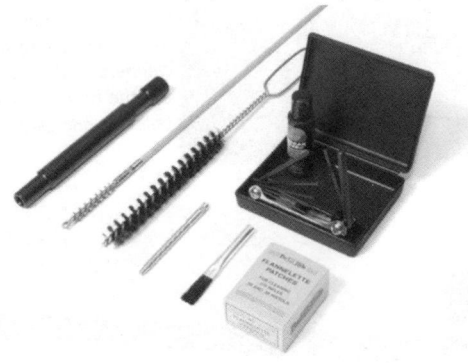

CAMOUFLAGE AND CONCEALMENT

INTRODUCTION
Camouflage and concealment are key skills for the sniper in the field. By mastering this skill, you will make yourself harder to detect and therefore harder to be acquired and engaged as a target. Ultimately it can save your life and attention to this skill will increase the survivability of the sniper pair.

Finally, you need to balance your camouflage with the ability to move without restriction, access your equipment and use your weapon and optics.

THE AIM OF CAMOUFLAGE
The aim of camouflage is to make you blend with your surrounding, move unseen, disguise distinctive shapes and break the engagement cycle as early as possible. In order to kill you, an enemy goes through the process of detecting a person, identifying that person as his opponent, acquiring a sight picture and finally pulling the trigger.

The best solution is to prevent detection, if that isn't possible then making it difficult to identify and acquire you will push the odds up in your battlefield survivability. The sniper has a great advantage here, over the Infantryman, whereupon he can use the greater range of his weapon systems to assist in his concealment. Camouflage can be seen as working in three different ways:

- **Blending with the Background** The need to blend with the background is the factor that most people associate immediately with camouflage. The Ghillie Suit is designed to hide the sniper against detection at close range during a chance encounter. Although the ghillie is effective it must be used in conjunction with natural camouflage and vegetation

- **Breaking up Distinctive Shapes** The human shape is instinctively recognizable as are features such as a human face. To a soldier, shapes such as weapons, helmets and bergens are so familiar as to be instantly recognizable

Thermal Sniper Ghillie known as the "TiC Suit"

Effective camouflage seeks to disrupt these shapes through contrasting colours and breaking up outlines.

For the sniper the head and shoulders is the most prominent and must be disguised by blending in perfectly into the surrounding terrain.

The use of a front and back screen will help to achieve this effect.

- **Reducing Signature** It is sometimes easy to forget that we also generate a signature outside the visual spectrum including human body heat, hot weapon barrels, mugs of hot drinks etc. Thermal signature can be reduced by operating on 'hard routine' when in close proximity to the enemy

Never fall into the trap of assuming that your enemy does not have a night vision capability. Assume that even irregular combatants from the developing world may have acquired such equipment.

WHY THINGS ARE SEEN

Whether an object is easy or difficult to see with either the naked eye or binoculars depends upon several factors. They can be remembered as the **'Seven Ss'**:

Shape Some things can be recognized instantly by their shape, particularly if they contrast with their surroundings. Two easily distinguished shapes which require disguise for concealment are: The clear cut shape of a soldier's outline and the smooth round top of a combat helmet/headdress.

Silhouette Any object silhouetted against a contrasting background is clearly visible. Smooth flat backgrounds such as water, a field, or worst of all the sky, should be considered dangerous. An object may also be silhouetted if it is against the background of another colour.

For concealment, choose an uneven background such as a hedge, bush, trees or broken ground.

Notice how the scope of this rifle is reflecting the light and will betray the snipers location

Shine. If an object has a texture that contrasts with its surroundings it is clearly visible. The surface of the combat helmet and white skin contrast violently with most backgrounds and need to be disguised to assist concealment.

Be aware of items that glint in sunlight which can be seen from long distances, the most likely cause of this for the sniper being the front lens of the riflescope. For the sniper this is simply called the "scope ring."

Shadow In sunlight, an object casts a shadow which gives away its presence. For concealment, keep in the shade if possible. The shade affords cover and there are no 'tell-tale' shadows. Remember that as the sun moves, so do the shadows. Trap shadow, such as in wooded areas, offers the sniper the best form of concealment.

Spacing Natural objects are never regularly spaced. Regular spacing means man-made objects. For concealment avoid regular spacing, although this is not really a problem for the sniper pair.

Sudden Movement The eye is attracted to any movement but especially sudden movement. For concealment, movement has to be slow and cautious.

Signature People, vehicles and equipment all have a Thermal Signature. While camouflaged in every other way, it is possible to see heat sources such as an engine block, a hot gun barrel, Hexi stove and a human body when using a Thermal Imager.

Equipment and dress also have different levels of Infra-Red reflectivity. Issued equipment has all been tested to minimise such signature.

Weapon Signature The traditional tell tale flash and muzzle blast are efficiently hidden by snipers using the tactical suppressor. The blast and flash weapon signature is still one of the biggest causes of detection and is one of the biggest reasons why the firer is seen, especially in low light or in the dark.

Basic Sniper Camouflage Techniques in 1916

THE GHILLIE JACKET

The name was derived from Scottish name "Gillie" which was especially used to refer to those assisting in deer stalking. The ghillie suit was developed by Scottish gamekeepers as a portable hunting suit/hide and was first worn as a military garment in 1916.

THE GHILLIE SHROUD

Purchased commercially the shroud is not only inexpensive but lightweight and far more suitable than the ghillie jacket. A typical design will have short sleeves and will be of a cape like appearance with small sections of elastic covering the surface. The detachable hood is very useful.

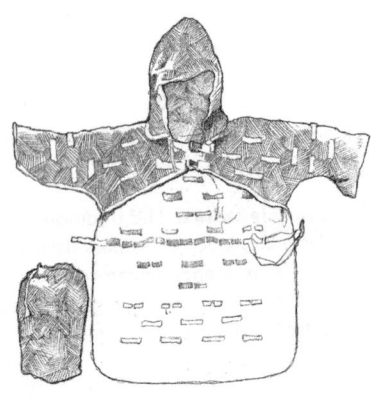

MAKING UP THE GHILLIE SUIT

Hessian/Burlap is cut into small strips of around 4-6 inches in length and attached to the shroud or jacket by using either glue or

sewing. Once in place different shades of hessian are attached and the brushed with a wire brush to remove the straight cut edges. The end result is a soft looking surface with no straight edges that can be detected by binoculars.

Build up the surface of the ghillie jacket by adding different shades and by a good wire brushing. The final result is shown on the right. All that is needed now is natural camouflage to be added to the elastic ties dependent upon the terrain being crossed.

STALKING

There are two reasons for the sniper stalk. Primarily aggressive operations utilising precision fire and also as a way of gathering live time reports and intelligence on the enemy, this sniper can offer this both by day and night.

Before the stalk the following
information must be obtained:
Known enemy locations.

- Target location
- Final Fire Position (FFP) and an alternate
- Routes in/out and alternatives
- Time on target, including duration of the task
- Firing window (time allotted for engagement) if employed

It is better known as :
- **E** : Enemy location
- **L** : Lines of advance
- **F** : Final fire position

THE DRAG BAG
Commonly used by some units during the stalk, it allows the sniper to advance armed with maximum firepower and offers some protection to the sniper rifle.

PLANNING
The following should be used to gather intelligence on both the enemy and the route before leaving on task:
- Maximum use of available air photos and maps
- Dead ground study (stereoscopy)
- Planning on 1:25,000 maps rather than the standard issue
- Previous patrol reports/first hand info of the ground relevant to task

ACTION ON THE STALK
The following should be kept in mind during a stalk:
- The type of movement
- Personal camouflage
- Maintain direction
- Alertness
- Observation
- Exposure
- Risks
- Dead ground

TYPES OF COVER EN ROUTE TO YOUR FFP
If possible use the following to the maximum to achieve your aim:
- Dead ground
- Streams and ditches
- Hedges and bushes and woods

ROUTE SELECTION
Keep the following in mind when selecting your route to your FFP:
- Observation
- Obstacles to movement(streams, roads and open ground)
- Dead ground
- Escape routes
- Time appreciation
- Best route(not always the best option)
- Position of FFP and alternate
- Where to move quickly in case of compromise
- Distant landmarks to aid navigation
- Move in bounds

PRINCIPLES EFFECTING MOVEMENT.

They are the following:
- **P** - Ploughed fields.
- **W** - Wildlife.
- **C** - Camouflage.
- **A** - Action in the FFP.
- **M** - Movement.
- **D** - Direction changes.
- **R** - Road and tracks.
- **A** - Advantages of noise.
- **S** - Steep and forward slopes.
- **S** - Silhouette.

WITHDRAWAL/EXTRACTION

Remember the following:
- Extraction plan
- Personal cam- change from bound to bound.
- Ground Sign
- No enemy follow up

HIDES

SNIPER SPECIFIC SURFACE HIDE
Elements specific to the construction of Sniper Surface OPs are as follows:

THE BELLY HIDE:
This type of hide is best used in a mobile scenario, or when the sniper pair do not intend to be in position for any more than 24hrs.

Advantages: Due to the small amount of digging involved the hide is easy and fairly quick to construct. This offers you the mobility factor as depending on the scenario you could possibly have pre dug positions ready to fall back into on a type of delaying task.

Disadvantages: Due to only having enough space to crawl in and out of the hide, and the fact that the whole of your time will be spent on your belly hence the name, this renders the hide very uncomfortable and should only be occupied for no more than 24hrs at a time.

This type of hide only gives a very small amount of protection from the natural elements. De-turf the shaped area marking out your loopholes, an old tin can is a good piece of equipment to use for this. Make sure that the turfs are kept as close to their natural shape as possible and placed down grass to grass spoil to spoil.

Construction: Once the area has been chosen you must avoid any movement to the front of your hide, so as not to disturb any of the natural foliage and place out a sentry for local protection, as these sort of hides at times will be constructed under the enemies noses.

Dig one foot below the surface level and long enough for the longest man in the pair, with good entry and exit point at the rear. The spoil must be placed onto a poncho away from the area of the hide to avoid any ground sign and can be reused later in the process for sandbags.

Over head cover should be placed on top; this could be built from old bits of wood that may be lying around the area to act as the main weight support. Next, place a poncho over the bits of wood. Peg down the poncho and replace the dugout spoil and then replace the natural foliage that was de-turfed.

Make both the entry and exit point at the rear of the hide, covered over with a screen and natural foliage.

SUB-SURFACE HIDES

The hide may have to be dug in when there is not enough cover to construct a surface OP or the sighting of the location is on a forward slope or linear feature, especially if there is a danger from indirect fire.

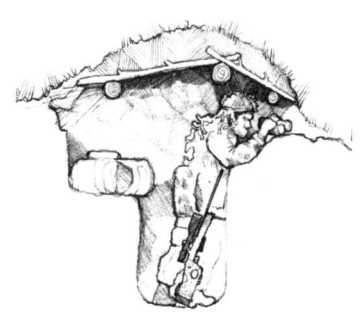

The following should be considered:
- What is to be done with the left over spoil?
- What equipment is available for supporting overhead cover?
- Time available for digging. (Modified belly hide or fire trench require approximately 3 hours digging)

The suggested construction sequence:
- Ponchos placed down to collect turf and top spoil
- Spoil is disposed of where it cannot be seen, i.e. stream or ditch
- Cross members placed across trench
- Top soil and turf replaced and area re-cammed

SNIPER SUB-SURFACE HIDES

There are two types of sub-surface hides that snipers use, these are the enlarged fire trench and the semi-permanent hide.

ENLARGED FIRE TRENCH

This a quick position to construct as half of the work has already been carried out, due to the fact you are using an old fire trench.

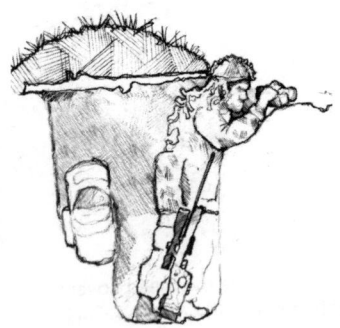

Advantages: Can be occupied for long periods at a time, due to the size and comfort it offers. Easily constructed by modifying an existing fire trench. Provides good protection from indirect fire.

Construction: The firing bay and the overhead cover are the only parts we need to complete this hide. The back part of the firing bay needs to be enlarged to the rear to allow for the length of the sniper rifle.

You must remember to also cut out your loopholes and your elbow rests, as well as the entry and exit point to the rear of the hide.

The overhead cover goes on in the same way as the belly hide, except more spoil could be placed on the top. Again care should be taken blending in with the rest of the fire trenches cover.

SEMI-PERMANENT HIDE.

This is the penthouse of locations; it is a well fortified bunker which really can only be built when you have time on your hands as part of the defensive plan, i.e. 48hrs minimum.

Advantages: Due to the nature of the location it will allow the sniper pair some comfort, thus allowing the pair to occupy the location for longer periods. This type of construction will give you good cover from enemy fire.

It will be constructed in such a way as to allow the occupants to move freely inside without fear of detection.

Disadvantages: Because the hide is to be occupied for long periods at a time and possibly used as part of the defensive plan it is going to take a lot of time and effort to construct. With the amount of construction needed specialist equipment could be needed such as picks, chain saws and axes.

RURAL OBSERVATION POSTS

INTRODUCTION
Battle Group Commanders want the maximum possible information on enemy strengths, movements, positions and intentions. At our level this is gained by means of surveillance achieved by observation posts from relatively close range. To be successful and remain undetected requires sound planning and preparation at all levels and a high standard of professionalism and determination from the OP team.

DEFINITION OF A SNIPER OBSERVATION POST
A position of observation that affords good concealment from enemy view and fire and allows the use of Sniper Weapon Systems to maximum effect.

OBSERVATION POST ENVIRONMENTS

The secondary role of the Sniper Platoon is to act as an OP and produce additional battlefield information with the ability to call in indirect fire as necessary.

There are two types of OP for working both rural and urban environments they are:
- **Overt:** Overwatch positions
- **Covert:** This as the title says is the type of OP everybody can relate to. They can be placed into any environment and are used for all intelligence gathering about the enemy routines from right under their noses

TASKS

Tasking and co-ordination of observation posts will vary from unit to unit but the procedure for setting up the OP should be as standard as possible throughout all Sniper Sections.

This Overt team is using the powerful AW50. The .50 calibre can shoot out to great distances against a variety of targets and is often used against "problem targets" such as vehicles and entrenched enemy snipers.

They should be tasked to support the CO's plan, specifically the CO's assessment of enemy approach routes.

An OP screen may consist of a combination of the following:
- Close Target Observation Post. Observation of a specific target, i.e. Bridges, junctions or buildings.
- Area Observation Posts. Observation of an area of enemy advance, withdrawal or infiltration.

The following are Sniper Platoon Tasks:
- To cover gaps in defences, mainly carried out when the company has moved into a long term defence location, now this is more than likely to be as part of a standing patrol task
- Early warning of attack, this task is carried out as jointly with the last one or used even down at section level whilst the section has gone firm in a harbour position the OP gets placed out to the area of the main enemy threat
- To establish daily patterns of life, enemy movement and dispositions. Used in both the overt and covert scenarios. For the overt role the use would be for internal security operations, as these types of OP would be able to pick up quickly on anything out of place, thus preventing terrorist attacks. In the covert role for ourselves it is used to help establish the daily habits of the enemy in and around their encamped locations, building up the intelligence needed to mount any form of attack onto the target
- Adjustment of indirect fire assets. During normal conventional operations the OP can provide support through indirect and direct fire, so as a sniper you must know the procedure for calling in and adjusting fire missions onto a target area

OBSERVATION POST SELECTION

To ensure the OP is successful and not compromised it *must have* the following points applied, without them there is a high possibility of aggressive compromise.

- **C - Concealment** – from the enemy from ground and air
- **O - Observation** – of the target area
- **C - Communications** – between team and base
- **S - Sustainability**
- **S - Survivability**

The selected position *should have* the following:

C - Cover from fire applying the principles of concealment you will prevent the enemy from viewing you position, however if by some chance the enemy locate the OP they will immediately start to engage you with at least small arms fire or at the worst case mortars.

Digging down will help to counter this and by using the spoil in the sand bags placing them around the observation, sentry and rest area will also add to your protection.

O - Observation of approach routes, if you decide to keep your sentry within the confines of the OP or out of it, he must be placed in a position so he can cover your approach and any possible enemy approach towards the OP site. The front approach will be scanned by the observation area.

C - Covered approach routes and exits from the FRV you come into the dangerous part of your occupation, where getting compromised at this stage will obviously blow the whole task.

To avoid this make sure your route selection is of the highest order so right up to the last moment you are in dead ground or out of sight of the enemy.

O - Observation over all likely enemy fire positions. Observation should be that large to enable the whole of the target area as well as the surrounding areas to be covered.

A - Alternative position, these need to be selected in the event of compromise. By moving into a new location you can still carry on with your task. Another reason why you will need an alternative position is if you do end up in the situation of not being able to see all of the target area you could use the cover of the night and move forward to a new position moving back before first light.

OBSERVATION POST LOCATIONS
Observation Posts can be sited in the following locations:
- Buildings. Barns, derelicts, rubble, houses and built up areas in general

Advantages:
- Ability to move undetected
- Comfort from the elements
- Protection from small arms fire
- Ability to stay on task longer (e.g. less hardship)

Disadvantages:
- Obvious location
- No escape route
- Unable to see approaches
- Extra manpower required to cover flanks

Sniper Fieldcraft

- **Woods:** Use the denser parts to give good cover, site well back to give depth. Avoid corners as they may be used as navigational points by enemy and friendly forces
- **Ditches:** Good cover from fire if not overlooked by high ground. May require a platform or duckboards, as they are prone to flooding
- **Hedgerows:** Most commonly selected location. Does not often offer good observation over all enemy avenues of approach
- **Brambles:** Often an isolated location. Difficult to conceal and usually a seasonal choice. Once occupied foliage is likely to deteriorate within 24hrs
 Rubbish Heaps: This will offer you plenty of cover due to the ability to use pieces of rubbish to shoot through. It is unlikely to offer good cover from fire
- **Vehicles.** Vehicle mounted positions are likely to be an exception: they are likely to be short term and contemplated only in circumstances of minimal threat.

Advantages:
- Movement between positions is quicker
- Communication from vehicles is better
- Quicker withdrawal
- Direct fire weapons readily available

Disadvantages
- Limited variety of positions
- Difficult to conceal against TI
- Lowers Senses
- Undetected withdrawal difficult

Areas to avoid are as follows:
A position that looks ideal to you as the sniper will also look the same to the enemy looking in your direction.

Stay away from any cover that is going to stand out as obvious to any enemy which they could use as a reference point straight onto your location.

Isolated cover should be considered in the same context as above, and finally the good old tree top, they are unsteady and hard to occupy let alone escape from.

ELEMENTS OF THE SNIPER OBSERVATION POST

Elements specific to the construction of Sniper OPs are as follows:

Loopholes - A loophole is an aperture made in the hide for the observation and firing under concealment. Loopholes should be constructed to give the snipers good fields of view and a good field of fire. They should be constructed so that they are narrow to the front and wide at the rear and have a cover to stop light from entering the hide when an entry or an exit is made.

Elbow rests - Sand bag to the rear of the loopholes will give the observer and firer good enough elbow rests.

Cover - The location should be situated in such a position so as to give the sniper as much natural cover to the front as possible, however this may not always be the case.
So the cover should be made up of the dug out spoil, logs that are around the area, ponchos to help water proofing and any de-turned sods.

Front and Rear appearances - The rear and front of the location being constructed should not be altered at all, and defiantly no movement should be made to the front of the hide during any stage of construction, so as to avoid any detection by the enemy.

The enemy should in theory be able to pass right over the hide without any suspicion.

Entry and Exit Points - These are the same point in the location and should only be large enough to fit a man. Once inside the position they should always be covered. You should never exit the hide without first making sure that the loopholes are covered over.

SURFACE OBSERVATION POSTS

This method is suitable for occupation in brambles, gorse ferns and other areas of adequate cover: Equipment: required is as follows:

- Cutting - secateurs, knives
- Digging – shovel, pick
- Supporting – chicken wire, ponchos, camouflage nets

The suggested sequence of construction:

- Poncho placed at OP entrance to reduce sign and remove soil.
- Construction party wear protective clothing if the OP is to be in brambles or gorse. Gortex suit is ideal
- Entry man lies on back and lifts hanging foliage and pushes into the bush
- Once inside, the tunnel is cut, ensuring that all the cuttings are kept inside
- Entrance will require a dog leg cut into it to ensure that an obvious tunnel effect is avoided
- Once cutting is complete, location should be concealed using chicken wire, ponchos and cam nets
- Thermal threat will indicate the need to dig down at least a foot and a wall of sand bags built with the spoil
- The spare spoil must be removed and hidden
- All equipment must be stowed inside OP

SUB-SURFACE OP

When there is not enough cover to construct a surface OP or the sighting of the location is on a forward slope or linear feature; especially if there is a danger from indirect fires the OP may have to be dug in. The following should be considered:

- What is to be done with the left over spoil?
- What equipment is available for supporting overhead cover (Ponchos, timber, IPK)?
- Time available for digging.
- The suggested construction sequence:
- Ponchos placed down to collect turf and top spoil.
- Spoil is disposed of where it cannot be seen, i.e. stream or ditch.
- Cross members placed across trench.
- Top soil and turf replaced and area re-cammed.

Elements specific to the construction of Sniper Sub-Surface OPs are as follows:

Advantages: Can be occupied for long periods at a time, due to the size and comfort it offers. Easily constructed by modifying an existing fire trench. Provides good protection from indirect fire.

Construction: The firing bay part of the trench is the part we need to construct this hide. The back part of the firing bay needs to be enlarged to the rear. Do not dig down as deep as the remainder of the trench as you want to cut out your sleeping shelf.

This will only be big enough for one man. You must remember to also cut out your loopholes and your elbow rests, and the entry and exit point to the rear of the hide. The overhead cover goes on in the same way as the belly hide, except more spoil can be placed on the cover, up to 2 feet making it blend in with the trenches cover.

URBAN SNIPING

The urban sniper utilises man made materials to assist him in his camouflage. Ghillie jackets take on more of the WWI drab effect and are supplemented by man made features such as painted lines on the shrouds.

URBAN OBSERVATION POSTS

During Urban Operations it may be necessary to site OPs in buildings. There are two factors to be considered,
- Firing Aperture. The aperture required in order to cover the field of view required?

- Firing Platform. Is there a floor for the position to be operated from or will it require building up?

FIRING FROM URBAN LOCATIONS
- The position should be kept for locating and observing targets, until such point that a specific target appears, as any hap hazard firing from the position will quickly lead to the enemy locating your position. When firing from the hide you should take note of the following points to aid in your position staying unseen

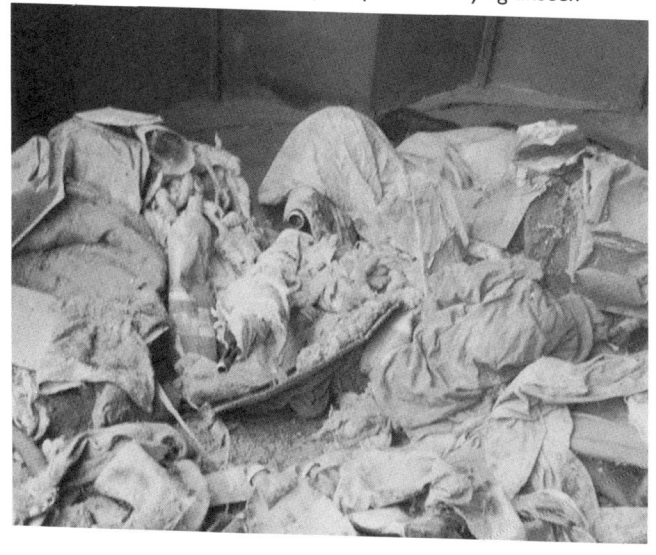

Flash can be seen at night, dawn and dusk, so care must be taken to hide this. This however should not be a problem if you construct your loopholes correctly and fire from the back of the loophole, which will keep your flash inside the hide.

- **Smoke** - Works in the same way as the flash, however smoke from your rifle will be detected on cold frosty days, so again take care in constructing your loopholes and make sure you are well back into your hide when taking a shot

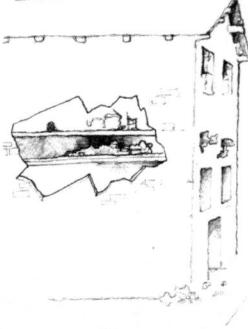

- **Dust** - One of the main places were dust will give away your position is when you are using a building as a hide, to counter act this you must dampen down your immediate surroundings by either pouring water everywhere or placing out wet pieces of cloth, especially underneath your weapon

This will also apply whilst inside your hide, mainly for the fact that once you've taken the shot the dust could engulf your hide rendering you useless for that point of time. Use of the tactical suppressor will normal reduce these risks.

DISADVANTAGES

- Due to the nature of urban warfare, it could be possible that the enemy attention will be drawn to buildings. This in turn could lead to the enemy turning the artillery onto them even if the sniper has not been detected

Points to note when setting up in a building are:
- **Preparation** - The building should be prepared in the same way as you would prepare a normal hide, the same attitude should be taken towards concealment as you would place towards rural hides. Loopholes should be built the same and your fire positions. You must take care not to alter the outward appearance of the building, i.e. not drawing the curtains, closing doors that are open, etc
- **Fire Positions** - The firing position must be set up so that it is kept back into the room with a screen set up to help place the firer into shadow

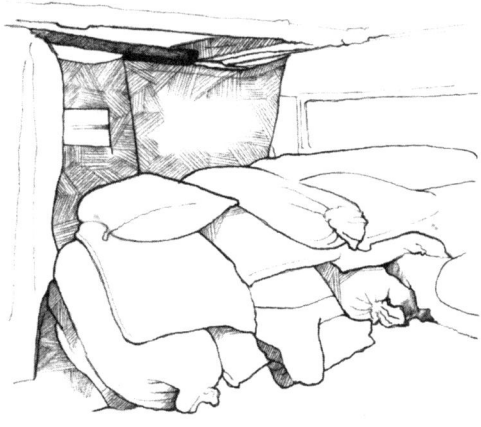

Sandbagged firing position, 5 meters away from the aperture, notice the floor cleared of dust to reduce signature and the hessian front screen that allows shots to pass through without deflection.

The loopholes are to be made the same way as for the rural hides, large at the rear and smaller to the front. These can be placed any where inside the house using such things as broken windows, shell damage to walls, from behind foliage that grows up the outside walls of the buildings, basically anything that can disguise your loophole can be used.

- **Observation Rests -** Some sort of observation rest for the firer and the observer will have to be constructed in order for them to gain much more accurate results. These can be constructed from old furniture that you will find lying about the house

- **Deception Measures -** In an ideal situation there should be a series of hides set up, which should be occupied under strict guidance, to aid in confusion to the enemy

Another good deception measure is the dummy hide, set off to your flank to help draw the enemy's attention away from your area and force him to give his position away. Lastly we have the tried and tested use of induced movement, this is done to working the same way the dummy hide.

A piece of wire or strong string can be tied to some obvious cover again away from your position and pulled at frequent intervals to draw out any enemy snipers and to force them to make a mistake.

Remember:
- Always assume you could be under observation of the enemy.
- Never be satisfied with the position if you think you can improve upon it.

Loopholes and potential dummy hides. Which one contains the sniper team?

VIEWING & FIRING APERTURES

The following are suggested aperture locations and methods of construction:

Gable Ends:
- Keep the hole small. Consider Night Vision and ambient light required to gain an image?
- As close to the eaves as possible in order to take advantage of the shadow given
- Scrape any mess forward
- If possible check area below for tell tale signs of fallen debris
- If in Defensive Phase consider tasking a friendly patrol to carry out a check on the concealment of the location

Slate Roof
- Use a coat hanger or piece of wire to secure tile from falling
- Large gap would be noticed during daylight hours

Making the Aperture:
- Noise will be a problem
- Hole must be large enough for the observer to see and use his weapon
- Good if task is to produce imagery only using cameras

Car Jack.
- It is sometimes possible to jack up eaves of a house to make a small hole.
- A normal car jack will do.
- Place boards under jack to stop pressure collapsing the ceiling under the jack.

This technique was use with effect during the Battle of Arnhem in 1944, by British Snipers.

SIMPLE LOOPHOLE APERTURES
Viewing & firing platforms
- Due to damage the flooring of the room being occupied could be missing or unsafe and will need to be replaced or repaired.

The following must be considered:
- Use existing boards that have fallen to the ground below. Make area large enough to move comfortably
- To eliminate the dead spot below the OP it may be possible to raise the height of the viewing platform, this would allow observation of the forward arc as well as the ability to look down

Back drop
- It may be necessary to consider the use of drops to reduce silhouette against the rear wall. If necessary they can be hung in front of to hide movement, giving a false impression of a rear wall.

SUMMARY

The sniper observation post is only as good as the snipers who man it. Good patrolling, selection, construction, routine and vacation will reduce the chances of discovery. The hardest parts of the operation are to find an OP and to build it.

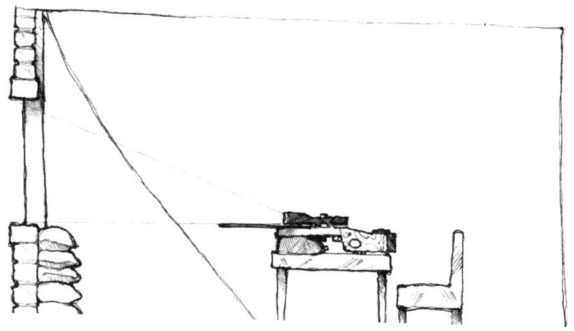

Living and working in the OP is very hard, both physically and mentally. Noise is particularly an issue that needs thinking about. When fighting the elements and fatigue, you must remain alert at all times, especially when the target area seems unproductive and quiet. Negative information can also be relevant and important to the Intelligence Cell.

Remember the OP is the eyes and ears of the parent unit, any piece of intelligence could be the vital ingredient to success or failure to the operation.

LOGGING AND REPORTING

INTRODUCTION
A Snipers secondary role is to gain information on enemy activity and movements so the information that he gleans must be passed on timely and accurate information.

THE OP LOG
A Sniper Section/Pair should always keep a log of all observations made during OP's or other tasks and feed them into the intelligence cycle by the use of a live/dead letter box.

The information in the logs is to be as accurate as possible, any opinions or unconfirmed information should be clearly marked in the log.

The log should be written clearly in capitals using a pencil as for radio logs and should be neat as possible. It should always be crossed referenced and clearly labelled with panoramic sketches, range cards and radio logs. Information that may be used by the enemy should be left blank until the section has returned to a safe location.

If working at night a Dictaphone can be used to record information and report completed when more convenient. Current information must be reported quickly (Live Time Reporting).

REPORT FORMATS
The Sniper section must ensure they all have report formats available to them for their tasks. These come in many formats but all can be found in TAMS.

Sighting Report: An easy format for the reporting bodies of troops is mnemonic SALUTE

- **S - Size.** The size of a group or unit that is being reported on.
- **A - Activity.** What is happening
- **L - Location.** Given as a grid reference, spot code, compound number, etc.
- **U - Uniform/unit.** If the actual unit cannot be identified then a detailed description must be obtained
- **T - Time.** Given as date time group (DTG)
- **E - Equipment.** Any specialist equipment that may indicate a various task or specialist vehicles.

INDIVIDUAL REPORTING:
When reporting individuals the A-H format is used:

- **A - Age.** The approximate age of the person between 5 year range i.e. 30-35
- **B - Build.** Stocky, thin, fat
- **C - Clothing.** Type, colour.
- **D - Distinguishing marks.** Unusual marks/scars
- **E - Elevation.** Height
- **F - Facial features.** A broad description of facial features
- **G - Gait.** The manner in which a person walks/stands
- **H - Hair.** Colour, style and length
- **S - Sex.** Male/female

WEAPON REPORT - CATS
- **C - Carriage.** Sling, wheels, tracks
- **A - Ammunition.** How fed i.e. belt, magazine, hand.
- **T - Type.** Rifle, Machine Gun, Pistol, Long, Short
- **S - Sights.** Telescopic, iron. etc.

VEHICLE REPORT - SCRIM
- **S** - **Shape.** A general description i.e. 4x4
- **C** - **Colour.**
- **R** - **Registration Number.** Full or partial
- **I** - **Identity.** Any distinguishing marks i.e. writing, dents etc
- **M** - **Make/model.** As much information as possible

PANORAMIC RANGE CARD
The panoramic range card should be clearly crossed referenced with the log with the use of vertical lines onto reference points or where the sighting took place. These can be extracted by either Live or Dead letter box, this will cut down the use of voice procedure and aid in timely and accurate information being reported back.

REF POINTS THAT NEED TO BE ADDED TO THE PANORAMIC IN THE INFORMATION BOX:
The addition of information into the boxes will aid effective reaction engage the enemy with either direct or indirect fire:
- 8 Fig Grid
- Magnetic bearing
- Distance in meters
- Elevation

LOGGING DURING DARKNESS
During the hours of darkness it may be necessary to use slightly different methods of logging. The following aides can be used.
- Dictaphone. Then after first light transfer all information into the log
- Exercise book
- Large writing
- Pocket memo

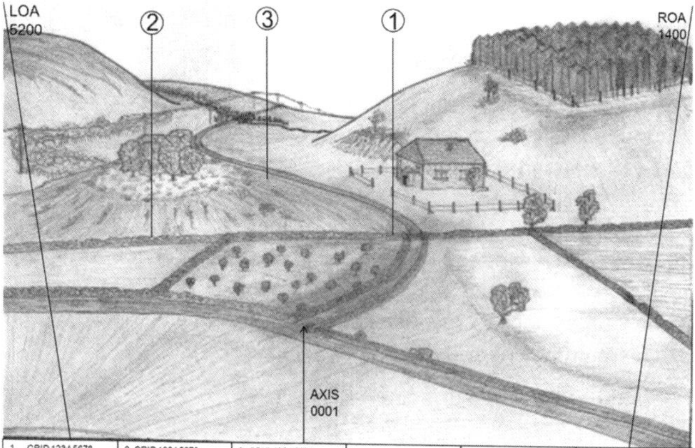

Sniper Fieldcraft

1. GRID 1234 5678 0800 mils mag 400M E 21	2. GRID 1234 5678 5800 mils mag 430M E 18	3. GRID 1234 5678 6300 mils mag 550M E 32			C/S 21E GRID 1234 5678 DTG 25 100 05 11 AXIS 0001 MILS MAG LOA 5200 MILS MAG ROA 1400 MILS MAG

SNIPER TARGET RECCE

AREA SEARCH
Before a target RECCE can be carried out, the enemy or their location must firstly be found and positively identified. To do this we must carry out an area search of possible locations.

Composition
The area search will require the whole platoon or section, until the enemy have been found and positively identified. This allows the Sniper Commander to search a wider area and then narrow his search when the enemy have been located.

The following planning considerations should be carried out before each mission:
- Map and Air photo study
- Dead ground study
- Pinpoint likely enemy positions using map/air photo
- Look for places where you would go
- Use previous patrol reports
- Weather considerations for patrol duration
- First light, last light, visibility levels
- Ground conditions
- Cache and FRV areas
- Routes in and out
- Timings, duration of task
- Day sacks or bergans
- Specialist equipment
- CASEVAC procedure
- SOP variations

Enemy force locations
- Strengths
- Type of unit
- Support weapons
- Doctrine
- Use of minefields/IED's
- Habits
- Morale
- Patrol activity
- Radio capabilities
- Viewing aids and surveillance devices
- Tactics

Friendly forces considerations
- De-confliction with friendly forces units
- Identify boundaries
- Location of own obstacles
- Location of own forward troops (FLOT)
- Support fire plan
- DF's (Allocated defensive artillery/mortar fire impact zones)
- Air/HELO (Helicopters) support
- Ranges of weapons
- Passwords/codes to be learnt
- COMMS plan (Communications)

Actions on locating the enemy or Target area
The patrol must know what actions on in the event of the following:
- Finding the enemy, reporting the enemy location, observe report and leave
- Compromise by the enemy
- Compromise by local nationals
- Sick or wounded man

- No comms
- Target not located
- Mission complete

Commander must know the following
- Mission
- Time available
- Size of force required
- Size of area to search
- Strength of enemy
- Location of friendly forces and supporting weapons

Means of carrying out a search
- Vehicles
- Foot

Methods of search
- Base line
- Cross grain
- Stream line
- Broken country
- Box fan

General
- Use common sense when planning
- Think about what type of unit you are looking for, where would you put it if it was your unit
- Vehicles generally move on tracks or roads and their hides are usually placed close by
- Certain weapons require longer ranges and can only be sited in certain areas to get their correct distance
- Always keep an eye out for sign whether its tracks or discarded rubbish

TARGET RECCE

As Snipers we do not need to involve ourselves with the typical RECCE Platoon type of CTR. We have adopted the same drills and procedures to fit our optical and observation capabilities which allow us to stand off at a distance and if needs be to also allow us to use our primary weapon systems to its full capabilities. Remember a target RECCE is a stalk from one position to another.

Conduct
- OP the Target for 24hrs
- Conduct a target RECCE
- Withdraw or conduct RV link up with relevant information

Phases of target RECCE
- Preparation and planning
- Target RECCE action
- Reporting

Planning considerations
- Time limitations
- Time of year
- Met Rep
- First Light/Last Light/Moon State
- Locals/Refugees
- Routes
- Specialist help
- All available intelligence
- Specialist equipment

ORDERS AND REHEARSALS

Commanders should cover the bare minimum
- Method of movement
- Action on objective
- Action on contact, light, obstacles, CASEVAC, lost etc.
- Method of target RECCE
- How many or size of group need for task
- Lost Comms
- Retrieval of information
- Maintaining eyes on target

RECCE action
The Sniper commander should deploy his section to best suit the weapon system and optics available. All target RECCEs can use the same basic groupings and these follow the same basic techniques as per RECCE Platoon drills.

- FRV party
- Cover group
- RECCE group

The commander can utilise the size of his section to deal with the target i.e. if he requires maximum barrels onto the target area, he can split the section into pairs and locate them to cover a wider area or arc. If he is required to cover one specific area then he can group his pairs together for maximum sustainability.

Methods of target RECCE
As already described the Sniper section/platoon can afford to stand off from the target due to the capabilities of his optics. But the sniper section must still be capable of carrying out a through and detailed 360 of the target location so that they can find the best possible locations to fire from. The best methods are:

- Right angle traverse
- Natural traverse
- Single point
- Static FRV, multi point
- Split Pair

Recording of information
It's important that all information is recorded accurately and can be related to the ground. Panoramic sketches may be used particularly if a wide view of the position is available. If map enlargements are used then the symbols used by the observer must be understood by all members of the patrol.

Modern pieces of equipment such as digital video cameras and Dictaphones can also be used as alternatives to sketches but thought must be given to how the data on the devices is to be retrieved and used.

Reporting information
Reporting can be done in various formats but the main way of delivering information will by the use of patrol reports. Critical information must be sent immediately if it is to be timely and accurate and of the use to either the Sniper Commander or Battle Group Commander. The following considerations should be used when compiling a report.

- The follow up may be conducted by somebody else
- The follow up OP may take place sometime later
- Reports must be accurate, neat and systematic
- A RECCE standard check list should be used to compile the report such as **(SLAMMAG)** or information such as Topographic details, Enemy locations, Security plan, Fire plan, Obstacles, Defences, Habits, Morale

S - Strength/ Size/ Dress
L - Location/ Description/ Grid Reference.
A - Aim i.e. Defensive position, Patrol harbour, OP etc.
M - Method, Routine, Tactics.
M - Morale, Attitude, Professionalism.
A - Aids, equipment, weapons, counter sniper measures, vehicles etc...
G - Ground, e.g. possible locations that can be used for friendly forces both in the RECCE and Attack.

The Successful Target RECCE requires:
- Planning
- Time
- Determination to succeed
- Professionalism and self-discipline

TARGET DETECTION AND SELECTION

TARGET DETECTION
The purpose of observation is to penetrate the enemy's concealment. To do this a highly developed sense of sight is essential, not only for the sniper to locate his quarry but also for his own survival

TRAINING THE EYE
- 20/20 vision perfect eyesight
- The eye is a muscle
- It can be exercised by observing over distances outdoors

MENTAL ALERTNESS
- The sniper must be alert to his natural surroundings and what is happening around him
- He must be aware of indicators that would normally defeat the casual observer
- Wildlife indicators
- Ground study
- Suspicious mind
- Keep an active mind

LIGHT
The light will constantly change
- A change in light conditions may reveal an object or position
- Position of the sun
- Exposed equipment may reflect light
- Clear light before and after rain showers
- Dawn/Dusk

OBSERVATION POSITION
- Not obvious
- Not near easily identifiable positions(corner of wood)
- Maximum fields of fire
- Maximum concealment

OBSERVATION PROCEDURES

GENERAL
As soon as the soldier arrives at his observation position he should commence to search the chosen area. To check for immediate danger a hasty search is carried out, followed by a detailed search. A range card should then be made out.

- **Hasty search:** This is a rapid search conducted when a sniper arrives in position and looks for likely enemy positions

- **Detailed search:** This one is a systematic examination of the snipers arc of responsibility broken down into a logical sequence i.e. near, centre, middle and far

MAINTAINING OBSERVATION
After completing his detailed search and his range card, the soldier must continue to keep the area under observation. To do this, he

should use a method similar to the hasty search but examine specific features in a sequence.

This will ensure that all features are covered. A detailed search should periodically be repeated. As soldiers will almost always work in pairs, they will take turns maintaining observation in order to reduce eye fatigue.

SCANNING AND SEARCHING
Scanning is a general and systematic examination of an area, to detect any unusual or significant object or movement. Searching is a thorough examination of certain features in the area? Both require complete concentration, combined with knowledge of why things are seen and the principles of Camouflage and concealment

SCANNING
Divide the area into foreground, middle distance and distance. Scan each area horizontally starting with the foreground. To obtain maximum efficiency, move the eyes in short overlapping movements. Moving the head will minimize eye fatigue. The speed at which scanning is carried out will depend upon the type of country being observed and the amount of cover it affords to possible targets.

When horizontal scanning is completed, scan along the line of any features which are angled away from the observation position.

SEARCHING

Searching may take place at any stage during scanning i.e., if the soldier's position is dominated by a piece of ground, he should search that area thoroughly before continuing with scanning

Furthermore, any significant movement or object, suspected camouflage, etc., spotted during scanning requires an immediate search of that area. The SUSAT/ACOG are useful aids when searching ground in detail, likewise binoculars. Other Aids to searching are the `family' of Thermal Imaging (TI) equipment held by the specialist platoons. Dead ground can be covered using remote control sensors.

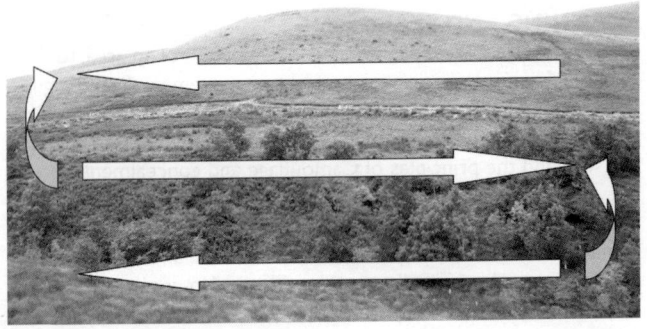

Search for each of the factors of why things are seen in turn. The weather may assist, i.e., frost will reveal tracks made during the night or a hot sun will alter the tone and colour of foliage used for camouflage by withering its leaves.

Search across hedgerows or a row of trees, not along them.

Judging Distances

In this detailed search the wooded area shaded in white is carefully searched after having scanned it from left to right and both up and down, nearest or most vulnerable ground to you, first.

The next area to be searched is the road (Arrowed) again from left to right.

Finally four areas within the black circles that could contain likely enemy positions are searched in depth.

Finally using the binos the remainder of the ground is double checked.

NIGHT OBSERVATION

NIGHT ADAPTATION

It takes the eye about 30 minutes to adapt itself to darkness. When a soldier moves to a place of observation at night he must give his eyes at least this much time to adapt before he can commence his move. Red goggles worn while in lighted areas will minimise the time needed for night adaptation.

OFF-CENTRE VISION

Off-centre vision is the technique of focusing attention on an object without looking directly at it. An object under direct gaze in dim light will blur, and appear to change shape, and fade. If the eyes are focused at different points around the object and about 100 to 150 mils away from it, off-centre vision will provide a true picture of the object.

NIGHT OBSERVATION AIDS

The following aids to night observation will assist the soldier in finding targets:

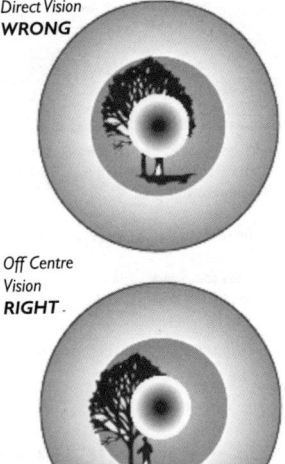

Direct Vision **WRONG**

Off Centre Vision **RIGHT**

- **Binoculars and Spotting Scopes:** Both instruments have some light gathering capability and will increase the range of observation. Lower magnification settings will draw in more light.
- **Image Intensification Devices:** These devices greatly assist night observation and can extend the range of the rifle to near daytime ranges.
- **Illumination:** Artillery and mortar flares, searchlights, even those of the enemy can aid the soldier, provided his night vision is guarded.
- **Thermal Imaging Devices:** These devices can greatly assist night observation of thermal images created by heat signatures of people.

DETECTION

The following are methods that may lead to detection for both the sniper and the enemy:

- **Movement:** The hasty search provides the best means for picking out movement

- **Sound:** Can be used to detect an enemy position and an alert sniper will hear anything that sounds out of the ordinary for the environment he is working in

- **Improper Camouflage:** Most targets on the battlefield are detected due to poor camouflage. However, many times an observation post or enemy firing position will blend almost perfectly with the natural background even with poor camouflage

  Only through extremely careful, detailed searching will these positions be revealed. There are numerous factors that can give away positions and these are:

  Surface/Shine/Glint. These may come from many sources, such as eyeglasses, reflective metal, optical devices, pools of water and even the natural oils from the skin. Shine may only last for a second, so the sniper must be alert to observe it.

  Outline: Most enemy soldiers will use camouflage on themselves, their equipment and positions. The sniper must be able to identify objects, even if he can only see parts of them or see them from unusual angles.

Contrast: Unusual colour stands out against its background, as does a piece of improper camouflage, e.g., a small patch of fresh soil or an unburied communication wire. While observing, anything that looks out of place or unusual should be studied in minute detail by the sniper. Curiosity will greatly increase the chances of spotting the hidden enemy.

THE CRACK & THUMP METHOD
When using the crack thump method, the sniper team is listening for the crack of the round passing overhead at supersonic speed and the thump of the discharge of the weapon being fired. This method will indicate both distance and direction to the target.

- **Distance to the Firer:** The time difference between the crack and the thump can be converted into an approximate range. A one second lapse between the two constitutes a distance of about 600 metres with most calibre weapons. Following this formula, a half second would be about 300 metres

- **Determining Direction:** It is natural to look in the direction of the crack. Instead, this should be a signal to prepare the senses to pick up the softer and less distinct thump, in order to determine its origin

- **Locating the Firer:** By observing in the direction of the thump and near the predetermined range, the sniper may be able to see the muzzle flash or blast of the enemy's weapon from a second or third shot

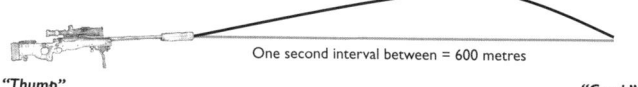

"Thump"   One second interval between = 600 metres   *"Crack"*

PERISCOPES

In static situation, periscope type devices can be safely used to observe the surrounding area. The sniper should not use these devices in an area in which he will be attempting to return fire, because they can draw attention to his final firing position (FFP).

SHOT ANALYSIS

If the sniper can locate two more bullet impact holes in trees, walls, dummy head, etc., it may be possible to determine the direction the shots came from by using the dummy head pencil method and triangulating in on the shooter's position. Of course, for this method to be accurate, all shots must be coming from the same position.

STIC (SNIPER THERMAL IMAGE CAPABILITY)

This can be used day and night to identified heat sources on the battle field making it easier to locate hidden positions however the ability to positively identify (PID) targets and individuals is reduced using Thermal Imagery (Ti.)

DUMMY TARGETS.

During WW1, snipers made use of Paper Mache heads as a lure to opposing snipers into shooting at them. When the head was hit, the sniper would place a pencil into the bullet hole, face the head in its original direction and from the direction the pencil was pointing, could determine the direction to the firer.

Today, the sniper can use this technique by using a Styrofoam head (as used to store fashion wigs on) and camouflaging it to look like a real soldier.

The sniper can put the head on a stick and slowly raise it into the enemy's view, as if it were an observer trying to peek over a berm or window sill. While one team member is doing this, another team member should be observing the area to catch sight of a muzzle blast or flash.

Judging Distances

METHODS OF INDICATION OF TARGETS

Professional soldiers train for combat action by practising battle drills. These drills are thought out carefully, so each action happens in the correct sequence and contributes to the overall success of the battle. Snipers, working in pairs, must communicate their thoughts once a target has been identified. Their battle drill for indication combines field craft and marksmanship skills and uses a sequence initialled **R - I - D - A - C - T**. The engagement sequence must be practiced over and over until you can do it in correct order, automatically.

R – Range
I – Indication
D – Deflection
A – Aim
C – Confirmation
T – Time To Fire.

- **Range:** Both No.1 and 2 work out the range to Tgt if time permits however the No.2 will generally work out the range whilst the No.1 is setting up his firing position. The No.2 has many aides to judge the distance either the PLRF-15c depending on conditions, Map, Bino's, spotting scope etc. There are two ways the elevation can be set either the No.2 sets the scales and the No.1 confirms or the most common way is the No.1 sets the scales and the No.2 confirms that they are set correctly

- **Indication :** The No.2 will indicate which Target will be engaged or the priority they will be engaged

- **Deflection:** Predominately the No.2 job to call the wind speed depending on the FFP, either using the Kestrel Wind Metre (WSM) or using the observation method, mirage etc. Once the

No.2 has direct called the wind speed to the No.1 will then set the scales with the No.2 confirming they are set correctly

- **Actual Aiming point:** The No.1 will always call his actual aiming point due so he knows his capabilities, the No.2 will call any corrections if required

- **Confirmation:** The team reconfirms all DATA has not changed especially the wind

- **Time to fire:** The No.2 will coordinate time to fire with either the Pl Comd/Sec Comd or for the pair. The time to fire may form part of an attack group Fire plan. If any change to the situation occurs, the No.2 will call **"STOP, STOP, STOP."**

TARGET ENGAGEMENT

It may be difficult to pinpoint the exact location of the fall of shot if the soldier misses. The observer has to use one of the following to assist him locate where the soldier's round has gone:

- **Swirl:** This is the displacement of air by the bullet as it travels to the target. Swirl is seen at the culminating point of the trajectory, which with the rifle are approximately two thirds of the distance to the target. The culminating points or Vertex Heights for the current 8.59 mm ball and API ammunition. An experienced observer will be able to track the swirl from culminating point to where the bullet landed. Unless the observer is directly behind the firer this will be difficult to pick up.

- **Strike:** This is the visible impact of the bullet hitting either the ground or a solid object near the target, or the target itself. The API round produces a distinctive flash if hitting a solid object.

Strike can be misleading if the bullet ricochets from the target or the angle from the firing position to target is not appreciated.

AFTER ACTION

Once the shot has been released the pair must continue to concentrate and follow out the following drills:

- **Follow through:** Follow through the shot without disturbing the sight and with no movement, no change in body or mind. The No.1 will re-cock the weapon as soon as the shot has been released. The No.2 watches the Target and observes where the bullet has impacted. If it missed, the spotter will give immediate corrects for the next shot however be aware you might not have time to readjust the scales but to hold off straight away

- **Engage other targets:** If there are multiple Targets all ranges would have been worked out before the initial shot however Mil Dot holds comes into its own due to the fact that it is only a matter of time before the enemy goes to ground. The Targets will now been engaged in priority order

- **Withdraw:** Once the mission is complete, withdraw as stated on orders, don't hang about to be followed up by the enemy. Be aware of indirect fire and obvious cover during the withdrawal phase as the enemy knows you are out there. Normally once three rounds have been fired the sniper pair should consider withdrawing from its firing position

INDEXING TARGETS

REASONS FOR INDEXING TARGETS
Indexing prevents confusion and provides a quick reference guide for locating targets. It also prevents indiscriminate firing which in turn could alert more valuable and closer targets to your presence. Since several targets may be observed at the same time. Indexing will help the shooter remember actual target locations and who they are.

REASONS FOR INDEXING MULTIPLE TARGETS
- **Exposure time:** Moving targets may expose themselves for only a short time. The Sniper Section must be alert to index points of disappearance of as many targets as possible before engaging any one of them. This will be extremely important when considering an ambush point and lead for a specific location

- **Number of targets:** When there are multiple targets the team must concentrate on the most important and exposed ones first

- **Spacing/Distance between targets:** The greater the distance between individual targets, the more difficult it is to note their movement. In such case the Section should accurately locate and engage the most important and often the nearest target first

- **Evaluation of aiming points:** Consideration is again given to working out where to aim at each target. A head shot has a higher probability of a miss than a full target exposure. A logical sequence is used to work out the best aiming points and thus identify which target can be engaged and in what order

BREVITY CODEWORDS FOR TRIGGERING AND ENGAGEMENT

The standard military practice is to allocate potential targets a prefix letter.

ALPHA	House, location, building.
BRAVO	Male (Each to be numbers ie BRAVO 1)
CHARLIE	Vehicle
ECHO	Female
MOBILE	Target is moving or on the move.
STAND BY	Repeated twice, used to trigger the activity or shoot.
STOP, STOP, STOP	Disengage, Weapons Tight, Target is Neutralised.

TARGET SELECTION

The Snipers Mission **"To locate, observe and destroy key enemy personnel and equipment with direct and indirect**

fire" The Sniper Section selects targets according to their value. Certain enemy personnel and equipment can be justifiable listed as Key Targets but their real worth must be decided by the sniper platoon/pair in relation to the circumstances in which they are located. Target selection will depend on the nature of the Mission. The normal list of priority is as follows:

SNIPER PRIORITY TARGET LIST
- Snipers
- Officers and NCOs
- Signallers/Specialists
- Crew served weapons (Heavy Machine Guns, Mortars etc)
- Equipment
- Optics
- Helicopters (On the ground or hovering)

CO-ORDINATED SHOOTING
At times more than one sniper pair will engage the same target. There may be a requirement to neutralise a High Value Target or threat. By using more than one sniper pair in this way increases the hit probability and often guarantees the neutralisation of the target. This is an area for individual sniper units to work their own Standard Operating Procedures (SOPs). The Basic rules to think about are:
- Sniper Ambush Effect and initiation of fire
- Deception
- Priority target engagement
- Multiple target engagement
- Range to target/s
- Planning and indexing
- Maximum rifles to achieve effect

JUDGING DISTANCE

THE UNIT OF MEASURE

Providing all the ground between the soldier and the object is visible, the soldier can use 100 metres as a unit of measure and estimate how many of these units he can fit in between himself and the object. Often we refer to this as how many football pitches we can fit it. This method is not very accurate for estimating distances over 400 metres.

APPEARANCE METHOD

The amount of visible detail of a soldier at various ranges gives a good indication of the distance he is away.

1. At 100 metres - clear in all detail.

2. At 200 metres - clear in all detail, colour of skin and equipment identifiable.

3. At 300 metres - clear body outline, face colour good remaining detail blurred.

4. At 400 metres - body outline clear, remaining detail blurred.

5. At 500 metres - body begins to taper, head becomes indistinct.

6. At 600 metres - body now wedge shaped, no head apparent.

CONDITIONS AFFECTING APPEARANCE

Objects seem closer than they are when:
- The light is bright or the sun is shining from behind the observer.
- They are bigger than the other objects around them.
- There is dead ground between them and the observer.
- They are higher up than the observer.

Objects seem further away than they are when:
- The light is bad or sun is in the observer's eyes.
- They are smaller than the other objects around them.
- Looking across a valley or down a street.
- The observer is lying down.
-

AIDS TO JUDGING DISTANCE

KEY RANGES
If the range to any area or object in an arc is known, it is possible to use that known range to judge the distance to nearby areas or objects. Key ranges may have been obtained using either of the methods of judging distance, by laser range finder, by maps or from targets that have been successfully engaged with specific sight setting.

Judging Distances

BRACKETING

The bracketing technique is a useful aid under most conditions. It requires the soldier to use the Appearance or Unit of Measure method to estimate the maximum feasible distance to the object and then the minimum possible distance. The estimate of the actual distance should be set midway between the two extremes e.g. maximum distance 800 metres; minimum distance 500 metres. Estimated distance = 650 metres.

HALVING

To distances of about 1000 metres it should be possible to select an area, or object about midway between the position and the target and in direct line with it.

Since it is generally easier to judge distance to closer objects, use the Appearance or Unit of Measure method to judge the distance to the midway area or object. Doubling this estimation produces a reasonably accurate judgement of range to the intended target. Care must be taken when judging the distance to the half way point as any error at this stage will be doubled in the final solution.

UNIT AVERAGE

When in a group, get each soldier individually, to judge the distance to an object using either the Appearance or Unit of Measure method. They can use any of the aids to judging distance that they are familiar with, but the judged distance must be an individual effort, because some will over estimate and others underestimate, their errors will cancel out. Taking an average of the estimates, an accurate range can often be produced.

OTHER DEVICES

Other devices which can be used to assist to judging distance are:

BINOCULARS: These are not generally available to all soldiers unless issued for specific duties. The graticule pattern of the binoculars can be used in much the same way as the sight picture of the iron sight or the SUSAT, to compare the appearance of objects or targets at various distances.

Practise is needed to understand and relate the size of the lines in relation to objects at different distances. The standard issue Bino has the following graticule pattern. Dimensions are as shown:

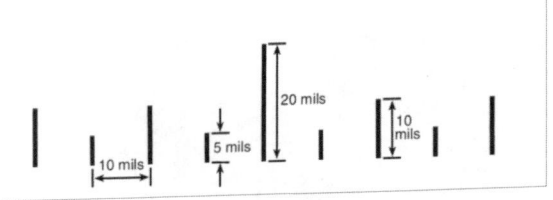

Judging Distances

FORMULA AND SUBTENSION RULE

One mil (MIL RAD) subtends a distance of one metre at 1000 metres therefore if you know the height or width of an object you can measure the angle that it subtends and calculate its range. Range estimations using the Binoculars and the Mil Dot system require two pieces of information:

- Known height of target in Metres (Accurate to .25 of a Metre)
- The estimated height of target in Mils

Once the two pieces of information are available a simple formula is applied to acquire the Range to Target:

$$\frac{\text{KNOWN HEIGHT OF TARGET IN METRES} \times 1000}{\text{RETICULE MEASUREMENT IN MILS}} = \text{RANGE IN METRES}$$

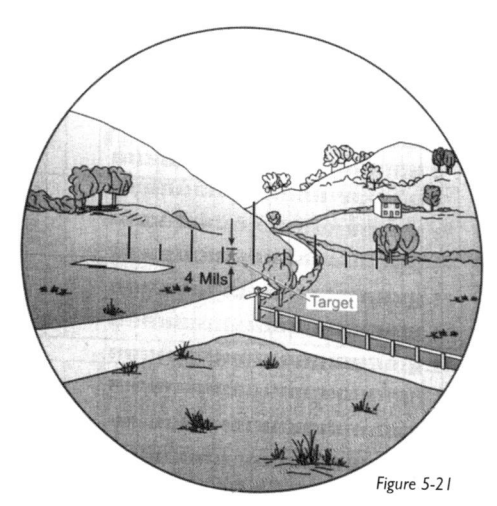

Figure 5-21

Judging Distances

In this case (pic on previous page) the target is an average man of 1.71 metres. He measures 4 Mils in height of the graticule pattern. Using the formula we get:

$$\frac{\text{KNOWN HEIGHT OF TARGET IN METRES } 1.70 \times 1000}{\text{RETICULE MEASUREMENT IN MILS} \quad 4} = 425 \text{ RANGE (in Metres)}$$

$$\frac{1.70 \times 1000}{4} = 425 \text{ Range (in Metres)}$$

Answer is 425 metres.

RANGING FIRE: When the tactical situation allows, advantage should be taken to fire at specific objects within the arc. Adjusting the strike until fire is correctly applied, then make a note of the sight setting used.

LASER RANGE FINDERS: The modern Sniper is now issued with PLRF-15C accurate to within 3m. The PLRF-15C has multiple functions it can measure the distance, distance between 2 points, work out angle range, take an azimuth bearing, measure angles and much more.

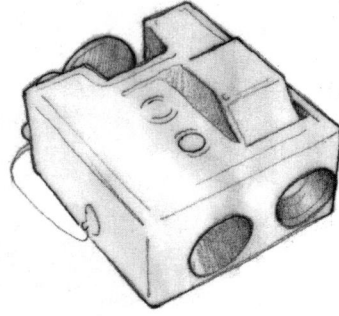

Judging Distances

MIL DOT SYSTEM: The Mil Dot system allows quick and accurate estimations of range without having to break fire positions.

The System uses the same Subtension Rule with the Mil Dots which are positioned on the reticule on the rifle scope. The advantage this has over the binocular graticules is that the sniper can remain observing the target and still range find. The Mil dot also can be used for aiming off for wind and estimating the aim of point for moving targets. The spotter uses the x40 Leupold Spotting Scope (L1A1) which has the same Mil Dot reticule pattern. This allows both to act as a team quickly whist engaging targets.

Although the system is becoming old fashioned it is still one of the most proven. A number of new reticules could replace the Mil Dot however it is universally used with good effect.

Remembering that 1 MIL RAD subtends 1 metre at 1000 metres, the 0.2 MIL RAD dots (Mil Dots) subtend 20 cm at 1000 metres. (or 20mm at 100 metres.)

0.2 Mil RAD

The spacing between the dots is 1 MIL RAD or 1 metre at 1000 metres (10cm at 100 metres)

The thick bars are spaced 10 MIL RAD apart.

So the formula again is:

$$\frac{\text{KNOWN HEIGHT OF TARGET IN METRES} \times 1000}{\text{RETICULE MEASUREMENT IN MILS RAD}} = \text{RANGE IN METRES}$$

Judging Distances

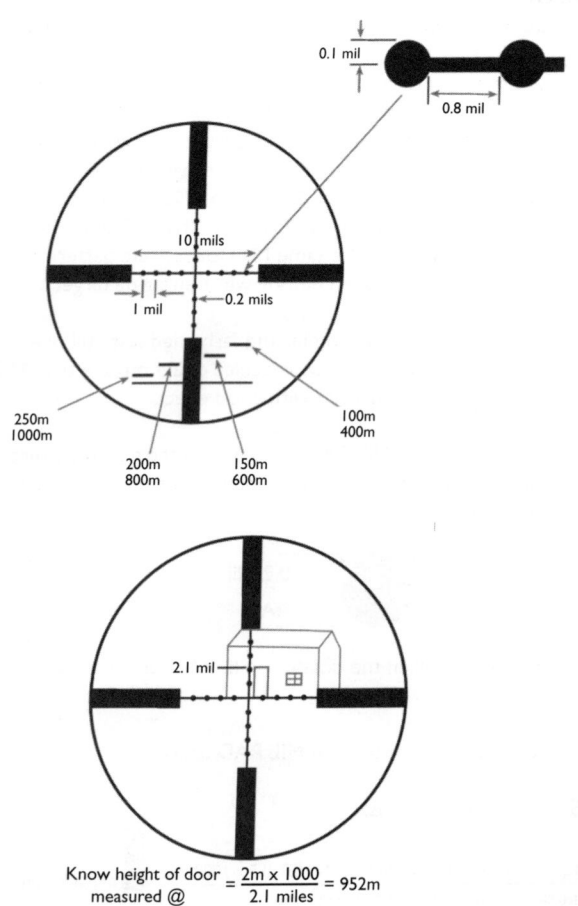

$$\text{Know height of door measured @} = \frac{2m \times 1000}{2.1 \text{ miles}} = 952m$$

Judging Distances

RANGE FINDING STADIA LINES:
Also allows a quick and accurate range estimation using the weapons sighting system.

The two range setting equate to a man's head and then torso fitting into the space between the steps, this gives an approximate range.

- Head Ranges are : 100, 150, 200, 250 metres
- Torso Ranges are: 400, 600, 800, 1000 metres

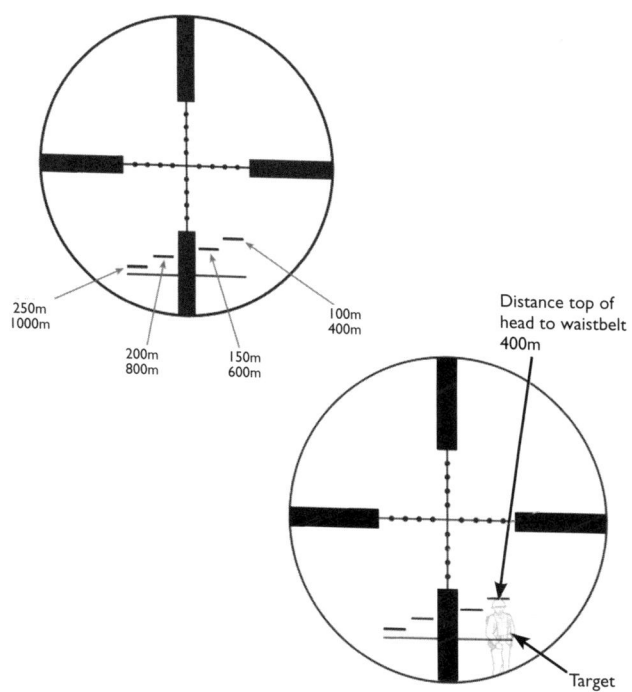

5 - 25

Judging Distances

CWS: Although rarely used by snipers today it still offers another method of range finding in the dark. The illuminated reticle gives the following measurements:

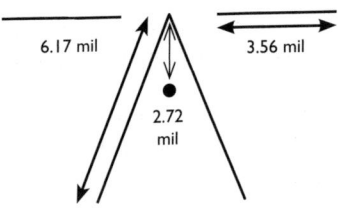

GPS: By changing a waypoint to the Grid of the En and pressing Goto will give you an accurate range to the target. However depending on how accurate you are with your grid and GPS signal strength may give you a wrong reading.

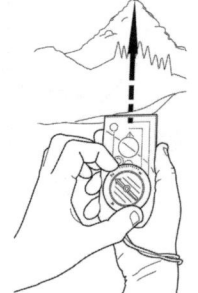

MAP: Use of a map measuring distances, is an accurate way to determine Short, Mid and Long Range distances.

However you've got to know your grid location and that of the target.

A number of aids that can help you on achieve this on the map sheet are:

- Ruler
- Compass
- Protractor
- Paper
- Watch

Advertisement

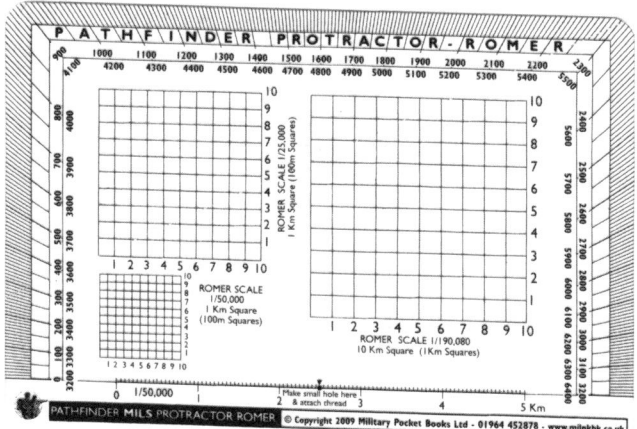

Protractor Romers available direct from www.milpkbk.co.uk

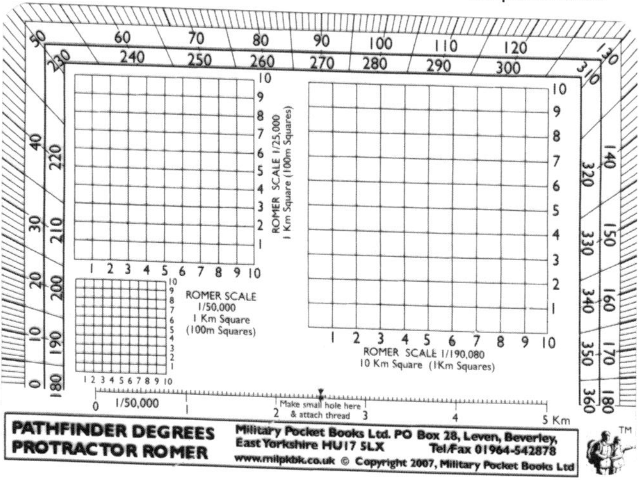

PANORAMIC SKETCHING

WHAT IS A PANORAMIC SKETCH?
A Panoramic sketch is a drawn reproduction of a view obtained from a given point.

USES OF THE SKETCH:
The Panoramic sketch aids the passage of information from one observer to the next within the OP. It shows clearly that targeted ground.

ADVANTAGES:
There are a number of advantages for using drawn Panoramic sketches, the obvious one being that it is simply done. However it does also give you the following:

- No requirement for specialist equipment i.e. cameras
- The information can be passed on instantly
- Up-to-date information
- Irrelevant information can be omitted
- Notes can be attached to the sketch to clarify details.

PRINCIPLES
Before sketching the following need to be considered:

- **S** Study the ground,
- **T** Top Third (This is how much of the page is left above the drawn Horizon Line.)
- **A** Avoid too much detail.
- **K** Keep in the Perspective
- **E** Easy Points – Left & Right of Arc, North Pointer, Scale Bar and Call Sign/Name
- **S** Shading where necessary

BUILDING THE PANORAMIC SKETCH USING THE PRINCIPLES ABOVE (STAKES)

Looking at a landscape and preparing to draw everything you can see in front of you can be a daunting prospect especially when the sniper is under pressure and maybe under a time constraint.

Before sketching we need to carefully study the ground and establish what the dominating feature is. It is also helpful at this point to determine the arcs of the sketch and to look for feature on or close to the arcs.

The next thing to establish is the Horizon Line. The top third is left free above the determined horizon line and the sketch is drawn like this:

Panoramic Sketching

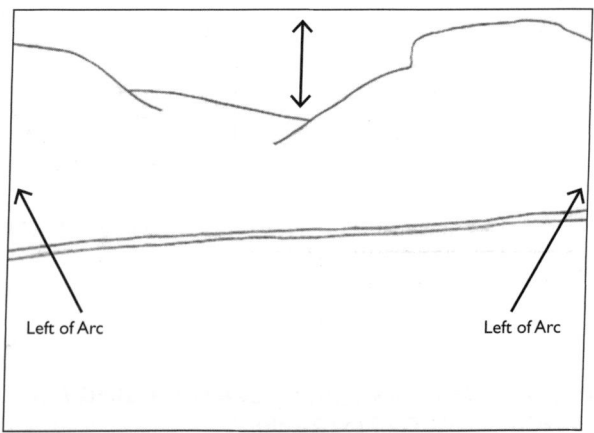

A good tip is to sketch the shape that you can see of the horizon. In this case the ground falls from the left of arc downwards to the halfway point and then climbs to a flat hill top on the right.
To assist in breaking this sketch into sections the main left to right road is drawn in. This splits the sketch into a top and bottom half and aids the correct composition

THE GRID METHOD

Another technique is to draw a Grid (bottom right). The sketch is broken down into grid boxes and each box contains the relevant part of the sketch.

The typical grid is simply based upon around 12 squares, four across and three down (below the horizon line.)
Whilst studying the ground you can also avoid too much detail by excluding irrelevant features or objects. Instead sketch on what is necessary and of tactical importance.

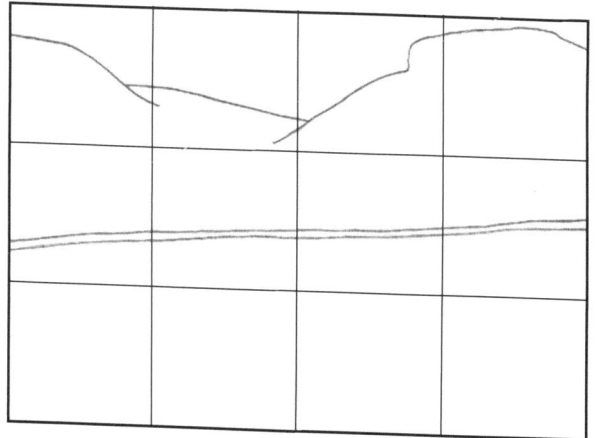

You are not there to produce a perfect work of art, rough outlines are perfect.

Remember the aim is to draw what you can see not imagine. Often the mistake is to draw with the perspective being from above.

Roads, Railway Lines, Fences and tree lines show how to keep in Perspective. In this picture you can clearly see how the sleepers get smaller as the get further away from the eye. The tracks start converging towards the horizon.

Detail like this is important and can be easily replicated into the drawing.
As long as the drawn objects gradually get smaller or converge the

viewer will get the idea of your perspective and this will give life to an otherwise flat sketch.

Simply by drawing the converging edges of this railway track will suffice without having to draw in each sleeper.

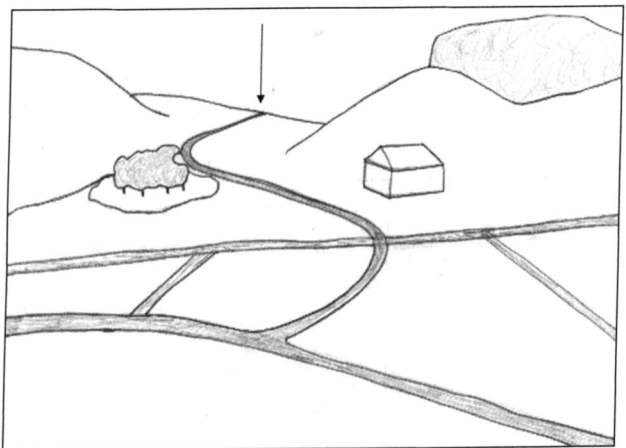

In this stage you can see that the extent of detail that has been determined as relevant has been included. The perspective is clear when you look at the roads. The middle road bends first to the left and then to the right before disappearing into the horizon (arrowed.)

This is called the "Vanishing Point". The sketch shows the viewer clearly where the horizon is and is accurate to the actual ground view. As a rough quick sketch the basic details are in place. To save time detail could be added by using notes describing of the features.

This is also the time to add the tactical information, the **Easy Points**. If time was an issue then at least the sketch would be both understandable and recognisable with these included.

The left and right of arc are drawn and at least one magnetic compass bearing.

The North pointer is normally an approximate Grid North direction arrow. A scale is added to the sketch by means of accurate measuring using either, graticules, Mil Dots or the map scale. This is best added to a linear feature such as a section of road rather than as a simple scale bar.

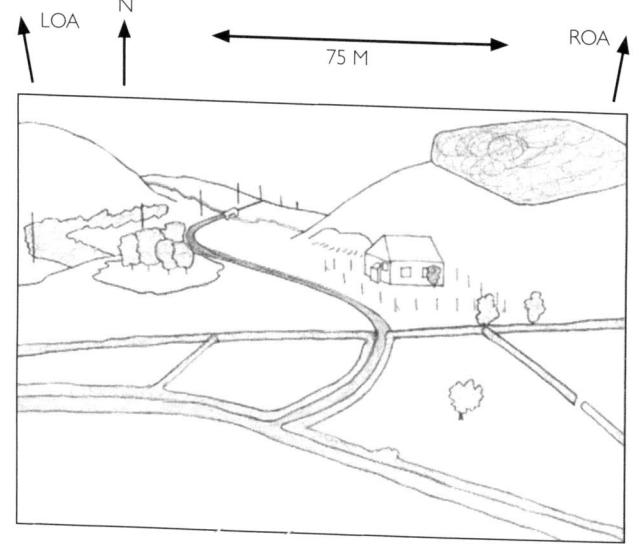

If time is available then more detail is added to give more tactical information.

Here you can now see the hedgerows flanking the road and types of cover available.

The building now shows both windows and the entry point of doorway.

Again important detail you would need to know if the sketch was to be used to plan an attack.

For the sniper commander the basic sketched details now enable the target areas to be indexed.
The windows of the house can be given numbers or individual names and the sides could be colour coded like this example:

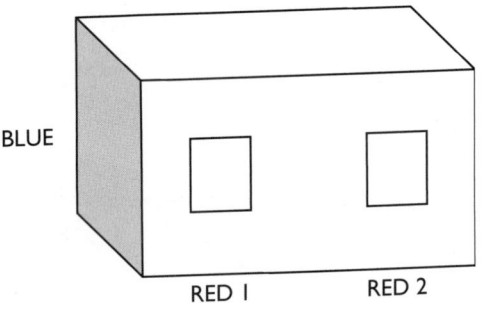

ADDING DETAIL AND SHADING

By using ordinary pencils the shading effect can really bring the sketch to life. The sketch has more of a three dimensional effect to it and the slopes and gradients can be determined.

A similar effect can be used by using coloured pencils again they help by showing the different terrains and features by adding colour. If you cannot sketch very well then colour can be used to help.

The key of shading is to use the side of the pencil and make the lines in the direction of the gradients. Pressing harder will give depth by showing the areas of both dead ground and ground that is in the shadows. By shading one corner of a building darker than the other will bring it to life.

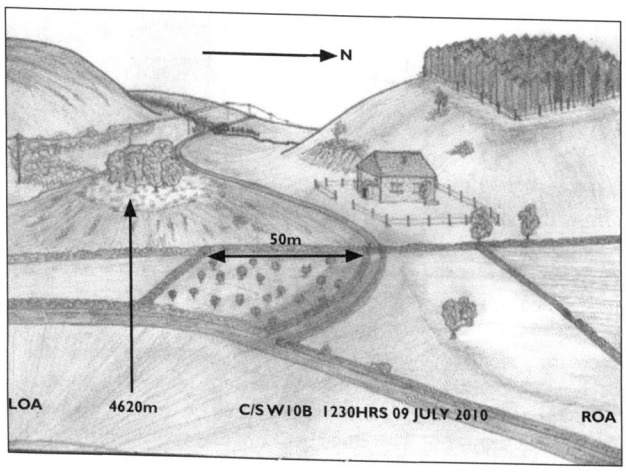

Shading may also be used to make specific points stand out more. You can also show an Objective Area in detail by just shading it and not the surroundings. This is called a "Thumbnail Sketch." It should include such detail as the Date, Time and the Grid reference.

Thumbnail Sketch – Objective Area GR 3561 5528 – 1630hrs 17 Jun 09

SUMMARY

Even with the advancing technology of Digital Photography it is essential that a sniper can produce a sketch that represents the ground accurately and can record important information which later can be used for intelligence purposes.

To create a Panoramic Sketch there is no need to carry any specialist electrical equipment just some pens, pencils, paper, a ruler and a rubber. Any irrelevant information can be omitted to avoid over complication and with the use of optics a specific area can be focused on.

This is an advantage over photography as the area may be too far away for a decent photograph. The information can be passed on immediately on the ground and can contain a Legend or Key to help in the understanding of the sketch.

The sketch can be linked to the OP Reporting Logs and by cross referencing can back up and support the information gathered.

For these reasons Panoramic Sketching will always be an essential skill for a sniper there will always be a requirement for this instant and effective method of collecting battlefield information both today and in the future.

SOLDIERS POCKET BOOK

Army Rumour Service - "5/5 a cracking little book"

SOLDIERS POCKET BOOK

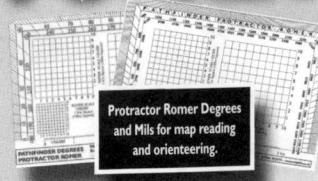

Protractor Romer Degrees and Mils for map reading and orienteering.

SOLDIERS POCKET BOOK — Available on the App Store

Android version

Military Pocket Books Ltd
Publishers of quality pocket books - online store

www.milpkbk.co.uk - Websales@milpkbk.co.uk - 01430 472087

also available from Amazon and Ebay

AIR PHOTOGRAPHY

INTRODUCTION
Air photography is probably the largest single source of information concerning the enemy. This is especially true in war-time when access to the enemy territory is difficult, if not impossible. Air photography provides a means of attaining accurate information quicker than any other source of military intelligence.

The use of air photography by snipers has its roots back in the First World War. It was and still is, used to supplement the map study and assist with the task of providing a picture on the ground of the most recent enemy dispositions.

USES OF AIR PHOTOGRAPHY
- **R** Reconnaissance
- **I** Intelligence.
- **B** Briefing.
- **I** Identification of targets.
- **N** Navigation

TACTICAL USE OF AIR PHOTOGRAPHY ON OPERATIONS
The greatest value of air photography is that they enable ground in the possession of the enemy to be studied in detail. Historically, ground that would be unknown behind the enemy lines can be seen from the air and therefore photographed. As well as military hardware and localities the topographical features of the ground can also be studied and used in the planning.

Air photographs cannot eliminate the need for ground reconnaissance but they can penetrate areas that do not allow ground observation. The photographs can be studied at length in a favourable environment and the results can both facilitate and speed up the ground task by showing which areas are likely to be of greatest importance.

TYPES OF AIR PHOTOGRAPHIC RECCE
There are three categories here:
- Strategic photographic reconnaissance
- Tactical photographic reconnaissance
- Survey/Cartographic photography

An example of the Tactical air photograph is a study of a precise area or target giving a number of angles in which the target can be studied from different viewpoints.

ADVANTAGES OVER MAPPING
Detail correct at time of photograph being taken.
- Exact measurement due to real items being measured.
- Greater Detail
- Shows Seasonal Change
- Height of objects can be determined
- North can be easily plotted

In this case the low flying aircraft photographed the tgt from a Low Oblique Angle giving accurate identification of military eqpt around the target area.

TYPES OF AIR PHOTOGRAPHY

The two categories are sub divided as Vertical and Oblique.

VERTICAL
The photographs are taken from a bird's eye view looking downward. With more than one camera on the aircraft a number of overlapping pictures are taken thus totally covering the area of interest. This is often referred to as Fan Vertical.

The sort of picture would look like this:

OBLIQUE
Again split into two types, High Oblique and Low Oblique.

High Oblique
Taken from an angle where the horizon is visible in the photograph. This type of photograph both shows the view from above and some profile and relief. Shadows can be determined assisting in determining features and objects.

LOW OBLIQUE

The photograph is taken by a low flypast of the target and gives the greater detail of a precise point or limited area. One of the first pictures of a German Radar Dish was taken in this way during 1941.

The detail taken by a low flying Spitfire resulted in a detailed scale model being made and later led to a successful raid that captured and the stole the dish for study by Allied Intelligence Analysis.

SCALING AIR PHOTOGRAPHY

The air photograph is measured and then scaled in a similar way to a map. Once accurate scaling is completed the photograph can then be Gridded. The reasons for this are obvious but this does allow unidentified or unknown objects to be scaled and measured.

There are a number of things that you need to know before you can scale the photo. The important thing is to know the height the photograph was taken from. Most military air photos include a "Titling Strip" that shows such details as:

- Height
- Date
- Time
- Photography Size
- Camera Focal Length

Air Photography

By using the Aircraft Height and multiplying it by size of the produced photograph the solution is divided by the Focal Length to give the Scale:

$$\frac{\text{Height 10,000 ft} \times 12 \times 12 \text{ inch print}}{\text{Camera Focal Length/Height - 6 inch}} \quad\quad 10000 \times 12 \div 6 = \mathbf{20000}$$
$$\text{or } \mathbf{1:20,000}$$

RECOGNITION METHOD

Another more accurate method is to identify an object on the photograph that you know the size for and then measure its actual size as it shows up on the photograph.

The sort of thing is normally an AFV or known military item that you can clearly see in the print. This will then give the height that the photograph was taken from and can also be used to scale the photo.
We know that point A to B measures 100m.
On the photo the object measures 5mm.

The formula is to multiply the know size by 1000mm and then to divide by the actual measured size.

$$\frac{\text{A to B} = 100\text{m} \times 1000}{\text{Size} = 5\text{mm}} \quad\quad 100 \times 1000 \div 5 = \mathbf{20000}$$
$$\text{or } \mathbf{20,000 \text{ feet}}$$

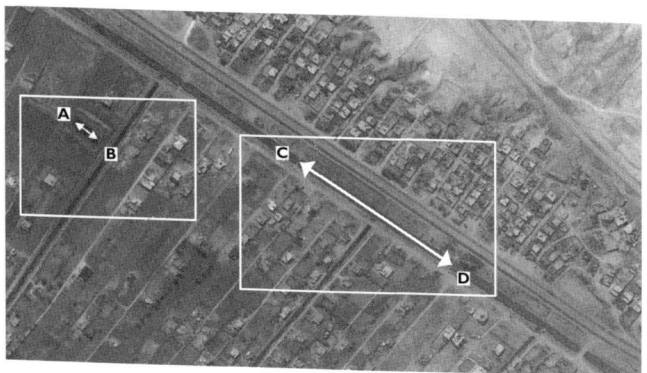

SCALE DEFINITION

Another method to help measure and scale the air photo is to measure the size of the object on the photograph and by multiplying it by the scale it will give you a fairly accurate measurement on the ground between two point.

In this case we use point C to D, bridge to bridge.

The distance between the two point measure 30mm. The scale is 1:10,000. Therefore the sum is:

$$\frac{30mm \times 1.10,000}{1000mm} \qquad 30 \times 10000 = 300000 \div 1000 = \mathbf{300}$$

The distance is 300 metres

PHOTO/MAP COMPARISON

Although similar to the Recognition Method a linear feature on the map can be quickly located and then plotted on the air photograph. A quick measurement can then be taken to produce a Roma that can be used to accurately scale the remainder of your air photo.

Ideally 1km apart on 1:25,000/1:50,000 maps the two points can be found on the photograph and this will give you the basis to make a Roma using Talc. The Roma is subdivided by 10 and each sub division will show you what 100m looks like on your air photo. With skill you can sub dived these again and make a Roma showing 50m intervals.

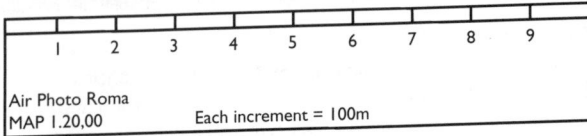

GRIDDING OF AIR PHOTOGRAPHS

To grid the vertical air photograph find at least two prominent points on both the map and air photo that are dissected by either a Northing or Easting line. Plot these on the air photograph and draw a line between them.

This procedure then needs to be carried out over your entire photo. This should now give you a grid over the entire area that relates to your map and as such grid references can be given by using your air photograph and the Roma.

You may find that the edges of some air photographs will cause the grid lines to curve slightly. This is caused by curvature of both the earth and the camera lens.

STEREOSCOPY

Stereoscopy is the term applied to science dealing with the 3rd dimension, height and relief.

When viewed as a single print many feature remain flat and are not noticed but when viewed in stereo (i.e. two overlapping prints of the same) the photograph comes alive and the following are seen;

- Gradients
- Rough heights of Objects
- Route Selection by ground study – you can actually see the ground in 3D.

Although an old fashioned technique some sniper groups still benefit from using Stereoscopes for studying air photographs

8 LONGEST SNIPER SHOTS IN HISTORY

Advances in technology have increased the range and accuracy of firearms and ammunition throughout history. Modern weaponry has made today's snipers the deadliest ever.

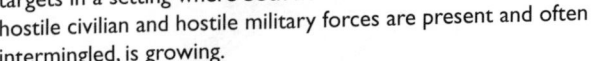

The demand for well-trained sniper teams that are equipped with state of the art sniper weapons systems and are fully capable of interdicting threat targets in a setting where both non-hostile civilian and hostile military forces are present and often intermingled, is growing.

The U.S. and its NATO allies have committed a considerable amount of funding to expand and improve sniper training over the past years. While seven out of eight of the longest sniper shots in history have taken place in the last decade, better technology and training are only two variables in the long-distance shooting equation.

Teamwork, natural skill and even luck all factor into the longest kill shots in the military books. The variables when shooting at distances up to one and a half miles can be staggering. It takes more than technology and know-how to tackle crosswinds, elevation and even the Earth's rotation. Here are 8 of the longest shots in modern times:

8. STAFF SERGEANT JIM GILLILAND'S 1,367-YARD (1,250 M) SHOT

Date:	September 27, 2005
Weapon:	M24 rifle Ammunition: 7.62x51mm NATO
Nationality:	USA
Military Unit:	2nd Battalion, 69th Armoured Regiment, 3rd Infantry Division Sniper Shadow Team
Conflict:	Iraq War in Ramadi
Specifics:	His shot might not be the longest ever, but it is believed to be the longest with the 7.62mm round. The 1,300-plus yard shot Gilliland made was with a standard-issue M24 rifle and a 7.62x51mm NATO round better known to civilians as the .308 Winchester, which is a popular choice among America's deer hunters.

7. UNKNOWN NORWEGIAN SNIPER'S 1,509-YARD (1,380 M) SHOT

Date:	November 2007
Weapon:	Barrett M82A1
Ammunition:	Rafouss NM140 MP (12.7 mm multi-purpose ammunition)
Nationality:	Norway
Military Unit:	Norwegian Army 2nd Battalion
Conflict:	War in Afghanistan

6. CORPORAL CHRISTOPHER REYNOLDS' 2,026-YARD (1,853 M) SHOT

Date:	August 2009
Weapon:	Accuracy International L115A3
Ammunition:	.338 Lapua Magnum RUAG Swiss P Ball
Nationality:	UK
Military Unit:	3 Scots: The Black Watch
Conflict:	War in Afghanistan
Specifics:	After sitting atop a roof for more than three days, Reynolds killed a Taliban commander nicknamed "Mula," who had been responsible for numerous multiple attacks on UK and US troops, from more than 2,000 yards away.

5. GUNNERY SERGEANT CARLOS HATHCOCK'S 2,500-YARD (2,286 M) SHOT

Date:	February 1967
Weapon:	M2 Browning machine gun
Ammunition:	.50 BMG
Nationality:	USA
Military Unit:	United States Marine Corps
Conflict:	Vietnam War

Specifics: A legend in the Marine Corps, Hathcock held the record of longest confirmed sniper kill for 35 years. The 2,500-yard shot was just one of the 93 confirmed kills Hathcock made during his career. At one time the North Vietnamese Army placed a $30,000 bounty on Hathcock.

But while every NVA sniper pursued "White Feather," the nickname given to him by NVA and Viet Cong due to Hathcocks habit of wearing one in his bush hat, none were successful.
The Gunnery Sergeant's military career came to an end after his transport unit struck an anti-tank mine. As of today, Hathcock is still ranked fourth on the list of most confirmed kills for an American sniper.

4 SGT. BRIAN KREMER'S 2,515-YARD (2,300 M) SHOT

Date: March 2004
Distance: 2,515 yd
Weapon: Barrett M82A1
Ammunition: Rafouss NM140 MP
(12.7 mm multi-purpose ammunition)
Nationality: USA
Military Unit: 2nd Ranger Battalion
Conflict: Iraq War

Specifics: With long-range shots in Afghanistan dominating this list, Kremer's 2,515-yard shot is one of two that came from Iraq. His 2004 shot came less than 150 yards short of setting the record, placing him just 11 yards behind Perry's one-time-record shot and giving him, at the time, the third-longest shot in history.

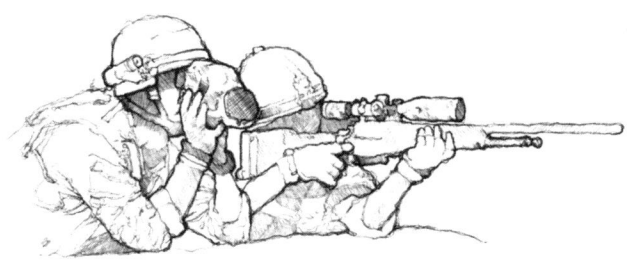

3 MASTER CORPORAL ARRON PERRY'S 2,526-YARD (2,310 M) SHOT

Date:	March 2002
Weapon:	McMillan Tac-50
Ammunition:	Hornady A-MAX .50 (.50 BMG)
Nationality:	Canada
Military Unit:	3rd Battalion, Princess Patricia's Canadian Light Infantry
Conflict:	War in Afghanistan
Specifics:	Perry held the record of longest sniper shot in history for perhaps the shortest time in history. Picking off an insurgent in Afghanistan in March 2002 from a distance of 2,526 yards, Perry bested Carlos Hitchcock's Vietnam-era record of 2,500 yards, but was quickly dethroned as the best long-range sniper by a member of his own team, Corporal Rob Furlong who made the second-longest shot in history, just weeks later.

2 CORPORAL ROB FURLONG'S 2,657-YARD (2,430 M) SHOT

Date:	March 2002
Weapon:	McMillan Tac-50
Ammunition:	Hornady A-MAX .50 (.50 BMG)
Nationality:	Canada
Military Unit:	3rd Battalion, Princess Patricia's Canadian Light Infantry
Conflict:	War in Afghanistan

Specifics: While participating in Operation Anaconda in Afghanistan's Shah-i-Kot Valley as a member of the 3rd Battalion of Princess Patricia's Canadian Light Infantry, Furlong witnessed and took aim at three Al-Qaeda fighters moving into a mountainside position with a RPK machine gun. Furlong's first shot missed the machine-gun toting insurgent and his second hit the gunner's backpack. The third shot from the McMillan Tac-50 struck the target's torso and killed him. At more than one mile and a muzzle speed of 2,700 fps, it took each bullet almost four seconds to reach the target.

CORPORAL OF HORSE CRAIG HARRISON'S 2,707-YARD (2,475 M) SHOT

Date:	November 2009
Weapon:	L115A3 Long Range Rifle
Ammunition:	.338 Lapua Magnum RUAG Swiss P Ball
Nationality:	UK
Military Unit:	Household Cavalry
Conflict:	War in Afghanistan

Specifics: Using nine shots to initially range his targets, Harrison and his spotter, Trooper Cliff O'Farrell, then dropped two Taliban machine-gunners with successive shots while providing cover fire for an Afghan National Army (ANA) patrol south of Musa Qala. Harrison noted that environmental conditions were perfect for long-range shooting: no wind, mild weather and clear visibility.

SUMMARY AND Q & A — CH 9

Snipers are a cost-effective capability, which when properly appreciated and employed by the commanders have utility throughout the entire spectrum of conflict. In other words they are an asset pretty much everywhere on the battlefield.

They have the ability to render elements of an enemy unit unwilling to move through panic and fear and cause a consequent reduction in the tempo of enemy operations.

This is only possible through the correct selection and training of snipers; the provision of necessary equipment to support their activities and, most importantly, a thorough understanding of how they should be tactically employed by commanders at all levels.

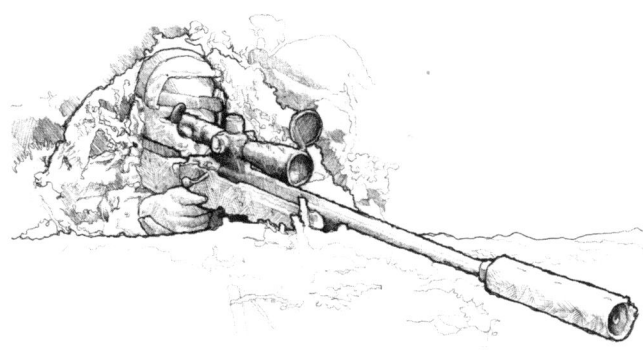

FRANK FLETCHER

Served a full career of 24 years in British Army with The Parachute Regiment.

Half of his career as both a Sniper and later Master Sniper Instructor.

His operational tours include Northern Ireland, Africa, Balkans, Iraq and Afghanistan.

Retiring in 2006 he now works in a similar capacity for Accuracy International, both in the testing and demonstration of sniper rifles and also training.

SNIPER QUESTION AND ANSWSERS

RG: Frank, you talk a lot about the importance of grouping shots, what sort of groupings would the sharpshooters of old have achieved with the Baker Rifle compared to today's shots?

FF: There is no real comparison with the technology available today. Armed with the right weapons, ammunition and training today's snipers can outshoot their adversaries by twice the distance. A typical sniper of today will put 5 shots into a 30mm group at 100m. At 1000m this becomes 300mm. That is something only dreamed of by the 95th Rifles. The interesting thing though is that although all this technology is available today you still have a man trying to outwit and outshoot another on the battlefield. That is something that has never changed.

RG: You mentioned that the Germans had 20,000 scoped rifles at the outbreak of WW1 and we had only 850, why did the Germans have 23 times as many?

FF: I suppose the answer here is lack of preparedness. I believe that this was the same with the Machine Gun. At first not really deemed necessary, but of course the Germans had plenty! The Germans had some fine hunting optics at their disposal and these were more readily used by hunters of the time so when the War started they were far better armed. The real point was that the British Army of that time was a small mobile expeditionary force of around 400,000 strong. Of these less than 150,000 were available to deploy to face the might of the 5.4 million strong German Army. Although the British Expeditionary Force (BEF) was a professional volunteer force it was totally unprepared to undertake large scale operations of this type.

Summary and Question and Answers

RG: Frank, we read through our military history books units being discarded willy nilly again and again, we never seem to learn, why do you think this is and do you think it will change?

FF: Unfortunately, Sniping is seen as a must have in war and might have in peace time. Obviously the Armed Forces need to adapt to the threat of the day but it must be remembered that war could happen tomorrow.

RG: You mentioned that the RM set up the first Sniper school, why did they get the jump over the Army?

FF: As an ex Para, I don't like to admit it but the Royal Marines have always held the lead in Sniping. This may date back to the days of Nelson, whereupon it was a Marine on board HMS Victory who shot and killed the Sharpshooter who had just shot and mortally wounded Lord Nelson at the point of victory against the French. During Vietnam the USMC was much better prepared for sniping operations than the US Army and this is much the same here in the UK. I would add that some sniper units are closing the gap though, on operations they are all equal.

RG: How does the kit that snipers carry differ from a normal Infanteer?

FF: The simple answer is that the sniper carries the tools that he needs to get the job done and as his work involves him being on his belly for long periods he carries less comforts. When it is man pitched against man simple extras like warm food and dry feet are not so important.

RG: Does physical fitness play a major role in Sniper Training as much as say in SF Training?

FF: A large part of the course syllabus is spent carrying loads over arduous terrain and the stealth part is equally physically demanding. A number of students fail each sniper course due to physical ability. Physical fitness and stamina is one of the most important requirements on all military battle courses.

RG: You mentioned that the Brits in the Falklands were often outgunned and out shot by the Argentines, how much of a serious threat were they?

FF: During the Battle of Goose Green, the snipers from 2 PARA were able to close and destroy their counterparts using better training and tactics. The big problem occurred at night, whereupon the Argentinean snipers were armed with far more efficient night vision and this enabled them to take out key personal thus causing section and platoon attacks to grind to a halt. An Argentinean sniper group on Mount Longdon held up numerous attacks on its key position until they were neutralised by both Milan Missile and bayonet. A good friend of mine was wounded when a sniper shot him in the mouth after he was identified to be a radio operator. He was fortunate that the bullet was off the mark by a few inches, and he continued the fight calling in fire support minus his front teeth!

RG: Frank, what do you think the future holds for the art of military sniping, both in terms of the technology and employment?

FF: Sniping continues to evolve and unlike other military thinking remains still unchanged. Even with thermal imaging and acoustic shot detection being used against him, the sniper still dominates the battlefield, using techniques to defeat both. I have also noticed how current operations have driven both rifle and ammunition design. Some much so that snipers are shooting almost 1000 meters further than they did Ten years ago. The way to think of sniping in the military is like being on a wave, at times right at the pinnacle of the crest and at others struggling to get back up. I would say that the business of sniping will be around for many years yet.

RG: What would you say is the ideal temperament for a sniper? What qualities do you look for?

FF: Firstly they are all volunteers, no one should join because he is told to do so. The two biggest qualities looked for are physical and mental strengths. Guys can be trained and taught to shoot but a hunting ability is a great asset. The sort of person who is looked for is a well balanced, quietly confident professional. Snipers often have a higher job satisfaction level than other soldiers. This is down to both the pre selection of the right person and the demands required to pass the sniper course. This self confidence gives them the edge on operations.

RG: Can you Parachute in with the sniper system? And if so what extra precautions do you need to take?

FF: With the robust rifle design that we have snipers can jump with the rifle and scope. Padding is always needed to protect the scope when jumping and this is removed on the DZ along with the Parachute. I would recommend carrying a spare rifle collimator for the team/platoon. This would give the snipers the confirmation that the rifle has lost not its zero without firing a shot. In practice the zero is not normally lost.

RG: What part of your sniper cadre did you find the hardest?

FF: Everyone finds one of seven skills hard. Traditionally this was the shooting and observation. Later when the L96A1 came into service this changed to the Observation and Judging Distance. For me the Observation was the toughest as I am a bit colour blind!

RG: You will have of course seen all the Sniper type films with Tom Berenger (Sniper), Jude Law (Enemy at the Gates) and Mark Wahlberg (Shooter), do they make you cringe or were they pretty accurate?

FF: I think that they all help with the mystique that is sniping. All have their pros and cons but the events are normally based upon real events. Did you know that the scene from Saving Private Ryan where Jackson snipes and kills the German sniper through his optic glass was based upon a real event that happened in Vietnam? USMC sniper legend Carlos Hathcock shot and killed a Vietcong sniper right through the length his riflescope when he saw a slight flash from the optic in the bright sun. He later remarked that when he recovered the body and rifle he realised that to have achieve this the VC sniper was aiming at him. It was just a case of who reacted and shot the quickest!

RG: In training you mentioned that as a planning figure, sniper pairs can be expected to provide eyes on for 48 hours, is this adhered to in practice or do they do much more?

FF: In reality the snipers will work the target as long as it takes. The 48 hours is based upon a pair operating on their own, providing a constant over watch of the target. The tactics of today allow more snipers to be deployed against perhaps the same target and that will not only give a greater close precision fire effect but will also allow a longer endurance period.

RG: Where does the actual tasking come from? You mention that the ISTAR Officer is responsible for co-ordination but who decides where the lads are sent?

FF: In my experience the key to close co-ordination is by direct liaison with the Battalion Commander. Snipers should work at that level (Battle Group) and have the flexibility to also work at Company level when required. The person ultimately responsible for sniper tasking should be the Sniper Commander working with both the CO and the ISTAR Officer. It takes time and trust but a good Sniper Commander should endeavour to aim at working in this way.

RG: I have been really surprised reading the transcript with you at how much detail and technical knowledge the modern sniper has to get to grips with. Have you noticed a big leap in the sophisticated knowledge since you first trained or has it always been like this?

FF: The amount of technical knowledge available today is huge. A lot of it is computer programme based and useful. I think that experience is far more important and that all the techniques and devices available do help, but the sniper should be able to do everything for himself by way of just the scope and rifle. At times the amount of information available can confuse so the old adage of "keep it simple stupid" works best with snipers. Electronic devices are an asset, such as night vision and laser range finders but too much technical instruction tends to confuse.

RG: Once you've trained as a sniper, how long would you expect to be in that front line roll? Do you think there is an optimum time or an expiry date? Is it a young man's game or is a more mature individual preferable?

FF: The thing about snipers is that they consider themselves to be of elite status, more skilled than their infantry counterpart. This of course is correct as the sniper course takes the infantry level of field craft and takes it up a notch. When a guy becomes a sniper he also gets the sniping bug! I have found that guys would rather pass over promotion to say in the Platoon. This indeed happened to me too! I don't think there is any age limit though of course the potential sniper should have served as an Infantryman for at least three years beforehand.

RG: Were you a natural shot right from the off or like the rest of us did you have to work at it?

FF: For me personally I think there was something already like that as I ended up in the Battalion Shooting Team at 18 years old. For sniping though I had to develop and refine my shooting ability accordingly. The great rifle design helped as I witnessed for myself the big leap that the L96 gave the snipers. Today I am still trying different things but would add that the key to long range shooting is having a stable platform, i.e. the rifle resting on the ground without human influence, and a good crisp trigger pull. Being able to read the wind helps too!

Summary and Question and Answers